It's Good To Be Alive Today

Margaret Lawrence

It's Good to be Alive today

Original version was published in 2008
Second revised print 2019

Dedication

To Alice, my Mother in Law, who helped me be what I am, with much
love.

To my Loving Daughter Ann, who is always there for me and without
her I wouldn't be here today

Acknowledgements

Thank you to all my family for the love and care over the years. A special thanks to my Grandson Stephen for all the work in getting this book republished.

Index

CHAPTER 1
My Birth Cover-up

I was born a love child, so I shouldn't be here at all.

I have a story to tell, so I shall begin at the beginning

My Grandmother and Grandfather fell in love and married when she was 16 and he was 18. She was a little dumpling of a girl who weighed 16 stones and had a lovely face with a gentle nature. My Grandfather was handsome, with a firm moustache. Their names were May and Alfred.

They had ten children, 3 boys and 7 girls. In those days large families were normal because there was no birth control. It was because of my Grandmother's fine cooking and good housekeeping that only one of her children died, a little girl called Olive, which my Grandmother was grief stricken about.

Two of her daughters, my Auntie Nin and Nellie, both met and fell in love with Bob who was much sought after by all the girls. Nin and Nellie both looked very much alike and Bob took to them both and used to take them out, sometimes alone and sometimes together.

He was made welcome in the family home and everyone knew that one of them would have him for a husband.

The girls were always nicely turned out, and looked lovely in their flapper dresses, with their rows of beads. They wouldn't dream of going out without their bright red lipstick on, sometimes they even put a little lipstick on their knees, just to encourage the boys to look at their very shapely legs.

Came the time when there was a big party and of course Bob took both of them. They had a great time and, not being used to drinking did the unforgivable thing in those days, they slept with Bob and he made love to them both.

Two months later, yes, both were pregnant. Bob now had to make up his mind which one, Nin or Nellie, was to be his bride.

There was a family conference with both Bob's parents, and the girls' parents involved, and after hours of discussions they decided that the eldest of the girls would become Bob's bride. That girl was my auntie Nin, so Nellie broke her heart and cried herself to sleep wondering what was to become of her. Nan hugged Nellie and cried herself, there wasn't much more she could do
to comfort her.

When Nellie at last cried herself to sleep, Nan went downstairs where the rest of the family were gathered and made them all promise not to tell a soul what had happened. 'Everything will be alright' she told Nellie the next morning. 'We shall look after you, and when the time comes, I shall deliver your baby, after all I have had enough of them to know what to do, and we shan't tell anyone else about this. When the baby arrives, I will tell everyone that it is mine, then you can get on with your life'.

It was 1926. In those days it was a great sin to have a child out of wedlock, so Nellie had to stop working when she started to show and she had to stay indoors and only go out at night for a walk or to get fresh air.

All the family kept the secret, they kept it so well that I didn't find out who my real dad was until I was twenty-one and married.

Nobody had much money in those days, and it says a lot for her mum and dad who supported her, she had no income whatsoever. The day of my birth came, 24th October 1926, no question of going to hospital. If the authorities had found out she would have been taken to a lunatic asylum, the child, me, sent for adoption and she would have been locked up for years. It really was terrible to have a child and not be married. Some girls went to back street abortionists, some died, some were damaged for life and could not have any more children, but not for Nellie with her loving mother to take care of her.

Came the day for me to arrive into the world. Nellie had a very difficult time, but she couldn't yell out with her pain because the houses were so small, and so close together, everyone down the street would have heard.

My grandmother delivered me and named me Margaret and fell in love with me immediately and wanted my mother to let everyone think that I was really her child. No one would ever know because if you remember I said that she was round and fat, no one ever knew when she was pregnant, and all her children were round, fat healthy babies. She pleaded with my mother for her own good to give me up so that she could carry on with her life and not be an outcast. How could she find someone to marry her when she had a child out of wedlock? I can understand my mother's feelings, don't we all love our own children, how can we bear to part with a child whose father we have loved and lost, and then have to give up that child?

So, my Grandmother could not have me altogether, but as things worked out, she might just as well have been my real mother as you will see later in the story.

Me Aged 4

CHAPTER 2
Surviving During the Hard days

We lived in a terraced house with six rooms and a scullery. We had no front garden, no back garden, just a concrete yard. The front door opened directly onto the street with the whitest step which everyone had to step over. Neighbours took great delight in keeping the front of their house spotless and it was the duty of one of the girls to do this.

We had an outside toilet and used cut up newspaper tied with string, no toilet rolls in those days, no bathroom, everyone had to wash in the scullery in a tin bowl in the sink.

The yard at the back held a big copper in which the weekly wash was boiled. Every Monday, firewood was collected by the boys to stoke up the fire under the boiler. There was a big wooden stick to poke the clothes with but first the dirty collars had to be scrubbed and the rubbing board, which was wooden with ridges in it, was put to good use. You must remember that there was no nylon, rayon, polyester or other man-made fibers, all clothes were cotton or wool.

In those days there was no electricity, we had gas mantels which were very delicate, the slightest touch and they would fall to pieces. We would not light the gas until it was really impossible to see because we had to save money which was very hard to come by.

We had a black range in the kitchen which was also the living room. This was kept alight all year round because it was used for cooking as well as being the only heating that was used in the house and always standing on the hob was a big black kettle. We had a gas stove, which was quite small, in the scullery.

The large family that lived in this small house, with its small rooms, included my grandmother, always called Nan, my grandfather Alfred, Nin, Amy, Maud, Nellie, Florrie, Emmie, Alf, Ted, Fred and Olive who died, my two cousins and me.

Friday night was bath night. Out came the large long bath, it was put in front of the range which always had a guard around. Our towels and clothes were put on it to keep warm, the bath was filled with buckets of hot water and in would go the first two smallest children, then the next two, each time topped up with hot water until everyone was clean - it was always nice on bath night because we had a great time.

Time for bed for the youngsters - five little ones to a double bed, three up, two down. We went to bed in our vest and knickers, the boys in their shirts, we cuddled up to keep warm for it was freezing cold in the winter.

When the wind blew it rattled the doors and windows, the wind seemed to find every little crack in the house to push its way in.

All the babies lived their first few months in a drawer. Just imagine only lino to put your bare feet on when you got out of bed, no heating even in the coldest winters, no wonder the memory of being cold lingers in my memory. In the mornings, we hurriedly got dressed and ran downstairs to a nice bowl of porridge.

Our house was in Lollard Street which led into Lambeth Walk in London. Lambeth Walk was a wonderful market street which kept open until quite late at night.
My Nan would do the shopping every day feeding 15 people every day with no fridge or freezer, it must have been a daunting task.

The boys made a cart with old wheels off a pram and wood from apple boxes which they got from the market. Each night after school the boys would go with Nan shopping. The butcher would stand on a box outside his shop and auction his pies, meat, sausages, offal and lovely dripping. He would shout "who wants this lovely joint for half a crown?" (A joint then was huge because most people had big families) - no answer so on would go a couple of pounds of sausages until someone bought it. The same thing at the bakers.

I used to love going down Lambeth Walk at night, every stall had lamps burning, the stall owners wouldn't go home until there was no one else to serve.

They would throw their empty boxes under the stalls, and if they were fruit and veg stalls, they would throw the produce that wasn't perfect into the empty boxes. This was a blessing to the very poor people, because they would send their children to gather up the best of the food, also the boxes for burning. The stall holders didn't mind, because it saved them the bother of getting rid of the stuff.

If you were sick or out of work, you didn't get much help from the government, in fact they would come to see if you had anything to sell rather than give you anything. There was no child allowance, no free medical help, you had to be nearly at death's door to call out a doctor. If you went to the doctor's surgery, you would have to pay a shilling before he would see you, then you were either given red medicine, or white medicine, which they made up themselves.

Nan sometimes bought some buns for a treat if they were going cheap, then the veg, but best of all the cooking apples. Nan made the most wonderful apple pies on Sundays. In fact, she was a marvelous cook, be it all plain cooking - none of the foreign food that we all eat today. I can never remember being hungry as a child, cold yes, but not hungry.

Everyone in our house had a job to do, boys and girls and woe betide anyone who didn't do their duty.

I can never remember that my Nan did anything except cooking. What I can remember is always being cuddled on her lap and her brushing my hair, she loved me, my Nan. When she sat down her lap disappeared. She was so fat and cuddly it was like falling into a feather bed. I was spoilt more than her own children. I took the place of her little girl Olive who died.

Nan and grandad always used to have a lie down on Sunday afternoon and the youngest children were sent to Sunday school, which left the oldest girls to get up to mischief. They would make tea, but Mum mustn't find out, so they used to top the milk up with water so that she wouldn't know.

I didn't see much of my Mum when I was small. She worked in a printing shop and most nights I was asleep in bed when she came home. My memories of my Mum aren't very strong, when I was a child, it was always Nan who was there for me, Nan I would run to if I hurt myself, it was Nan who cuddled me until I went to sleep.

My Auntie Florrie was ten years older than me and it was her job to take me out and look after me. She told me later in life that she was fed up because she could never go out to play without dragging me along. My Auntie Florrie spoke with a small lisp and so do I, perhaps she taught me how to speak.

My granddad worked all his life for the Gas Company, he used to wear his trouser legs tied up with string to keep them dry. His job was to dig holes in the roads, sometimes he had to sit in a little tent with a fire in the brazier, minding the hole.

Once he was working near home and Auntie Florrie and I took him his lunch and we cooked chestnuts on his fire. It was great fun. My granddad used to have the same lunch every day - bread and cheese tied up in a spotted red and white cloth then pop in the pub for a drink to wash it down.

Every night when he came home, he would sit down to his dinner which could have been steak and kidney pudding or pie or wonderful stew with dumplings which were all my favourites. Of course, we little ones only had the veg with gravy, lovely. I would stand by his knee watching every mouthful he took. He would look at me and smile and sometimes wink his eye. He would come to the very last forkful, look at me, then pretend to eat it, but I knew that last mouthful was mine and he would pop it into my mouth with a flourish. I must have been about two or three years old then.

Every Friday was pay day. In the kitchen living room we had a large scrubbed table and Nan used to put on her clean apron (she always wore flannel petticoats down to her ankles, a blouse and an overall which completely covered her. These clothes she made herself because of her size.

Nan sat at the table waiting for the boys and girls to come home from work.
They would place their unopened wage packets on the table where Nan would sort it out for the various expenses, rent, tally man, insurance (we were all insured for a penny a week to cover sickness and death bills) food and clothes, although clothes were not bought very often. Money left over was then shared according to the amount they earned, if the boys were courting they got extra.

The clothes were passed down, darned and mended, through the children.
All my clothes were made by my mother by hand from her sisters' cast offs. She would make me knickers and dresses to match, I always looked nice although none of us had more than one change of clothes and only one pair of shoes. I never had shoes, Mum used to buy me black plimsolls from Woolworth's, which was the sixpenny store, nothing was sold over sixpence, and my plimsolls were 3d each, 6d for the pair. This was how I was dressed until I was evacuated at the start of the war.

Some of these very old houses, which were all rented because the people couldn't possibly afford to buy their own, were running alive with bugs You see when the people put wallpaper up, they made the paste with flour and water which was like putting food on the walls for these parasites. Once you got a couple of these in your home they soon multiplied. They would get in your bed at night and feed off of your blood. It must have been awful for people that had them, because when you turned over in your sleep, you squashed them which left your bed stained with blood.

When I was three years old, everyone was out at work or school. I missed everybody - we had no toys, no radio, Nan was busy preparing the meal, so I started following my uncle Fred to school. He was 5 years older than me. I would go into the classroom and sit down with the other children. The teacher would find me and call my Fred to take me home. Every day this happened until the teacher decided I could stay and so began my school days which I loved. In the afternoon all the little ones were to lie down on small camp beds to have a sleep. Our teacher would sing to us - it was nice.

Saturday was my favourite day. Everyone was home and busy doing chores. There was the shopping down Lambeth Walk, whoever went with Nan to pull the box on wheels home, was rewarded with a toffee apple. I was only three years old, too young to pull the barrow, but I knew Nan would have an apple for me as a treat.

On Saturday night all the adults would go to the pub in Lambeth Walk -remember it was only down the end of our street. There would be the piano playing and everyone would sing and enjoy themselves, even the kids outside the pub could learn the words and sing. They would poke their noses round the door and their mum and dad would pass out the lemonade.

My Nan didn't like her little ones doing this, so we had a penny each to go to Burroughs, the pie and mash shop opposite the pub which stayed open `especially for the purpose on Saturday night to give the kids a treat. Oh, what bliss, mash and liquor smothered in salt and vinegar. The liquor was parsley sauce. When we had eaten, we were taken home to bed, sometimes we would be woken up because there was a party going on. I didn't know if it was a celebration or what because I was only a baby. The doors would be unscrewed and taken off to make more room and although there wasn't much furniture, they had a piano and usually a crate of beer from the pub. We little ones would creep downstairs and poke our noses through the banisters to watch all the fun. Everyone had to perform, to sing, dance, tell jokes and anything to entertain.

There were no locks on our house, we had a string through a hole in the front door to pull the latch open and neighbours and friends would pull the string, walk in and say "hello", so when a party was happening, neighbours would come and join in the fun, spilling onto the pavement. Everyone knew everyone in our street, they helped each other. I can't remember any rows or fights. Monday morning Nan would collect up the men's and boys' suits to take them along to the pawnbroker in Lambeth Walk where he would put them on a hanger until the following Saturday. Sunday was the day everyone wore their best clothes.

Ronnie, Albe and me

Wash day was Monday. When I was a toddler, the copper was going in the yard, filled with the weekly whites, the big iron mangle for wringing the water out was being put to good use. I saw the cogs of the turning wheel going around

15

and put my finger in whilst my Auntie wasn't looking. My index finger on my left hand was hanging off - panic stations as I was rushed to St Thomas's Hospital to have it stitched on again.

Everyone in those days got the usual illnesses going around because people lived so close together, so if one caught something, everyone else did. I remember I had whooping cough about this time.
Lambeth Bridge was being freshly tarred so my mother took me to inhale the fumes and watch the boats go by- it was said that the fumes from the tar would ease the cough, you didn't need to see a doctor for something like that, in fact you didn't need to see the doctor for measles, chicken pots, flu, etc. perhaps that's why so many children died young.

I was four years old; my mother fell for Harry who was a gentleman's valet. He was always dressed so smart (his clothes were cast offs from his boss). Mum went out with him quite a few times before telling him that I was her daughter, but he didn't seem to mind, and he asked her to marry him. So they got married in the Register Office and mum was able to register me as being born with a father's name on the certificate. My birth certificate is dated four years after my birth.

I continued to live with my Nan until we moved to Brixton. By this time most of my aunts and uncles had got married and moved away so we had a small terraced house in

Robsart Street, once again with no front garden - a small yard out the back. I hated the outside toilet, it was so cold in the winter, just imagine sitting out there with the snow all around and bare from the waist down, brrr!

One of my memories is of the street hawkers. There was the salt and vinegar man, great lumps of salt which he would cut a large pennyworth off and vinegar in a barrel. You had to take a jug or jar which he would fill for you. Then the milk man with the little pony and cart loaded with a large churn. He would fill your jugs for a penny for about a quart. My favourite was the rag and bone man. He had a little turntable on the back of his cart with a seat on. You would take out jars and rags and he would give you a ride by turning the handle. Then there was the ice cream cart which was only a box on the front of a three wheeled bicycle. We used to try and get a free lick because we couldn't buy one. He used to shout out "Come and buy one, lovely lollies and ice cream". There was the lavender lady who would call out "Lavender, who'll buy my sweet-smelling lavender, only a penny?"

The gypsies would have clothes pegs and heather and want to tell your fortune. On Sunday morning the fish man would push his barrow round the streets selling winkles, shrimps and whelks.
My Auntie Emmie would buy winkles and sit picking them out with a pin until she had a pint glass full, then she would put vinegar and pepper on them and we would have them for Sunday tea with bread and marge. My Auntie Emmie

was not very bright, she had got married but couldn't bear to leave home and Albert, her husband, didn't want to live in Nan's house. He wanted his own home so Auntie Emmie stayed home and Albert would take her out and visit her as if they were courting. She had three children, Albert, Ronald and Ted and we all lived with Nan. Nan used to keep Emmie away from school a lot when she was young to help with bringing up the family and to do the chores, prepare the veg and scrubbing etc. Emmie was always eager to work and would help anyone.

We were still very poor and had to watch the pennies. There was a lovely shop on the corner which sold everything. Nothing was nicely packed; it all came loose. They used to twist cones of paper to put the various things in, like flour and fruit etc. We used to ask for broken biscuits which were going cheap and Nan would sometimes give us a penny to buy some. The eggs used to be in a big bowl on the counter and often they would get cracked. We would buy these 13 for a penny.

As I grew up, I began to realise that we were poor. I had never thought of us being poor as there were so many people worse off than us but when you reach the age of about seven and see other children from school with their dolls and skates and books and yo-yos and other nice things, especially at Christmas time, you begin to want.

I wanted a doll for Christmas. We used to hang up one of the big boy's socks and Christmas morning we would find it filled with nuts, an apple, an orange and a silver three penny piece - but this special Christmas, because I was Nan's favourite, I had a doll. It was a black doll made of papier mache about 10" tall. I wore that doll out playing with it. We children would cut up crepe paper and sit for hours making chains to hang up for decoration, we didn't have a tree, Nan said that there wouldn't be room for one, but we knew, trees cost money, and we needed money to spend for Christmas. When Nan made the Christmas pudding, we all had a stir and a wish. Nan would put in some of her Guinness, she loved to have a glass of Guinness.

We always had chicken for Christmas. Chickens were not so plentiful then as they are now. All the family would come later in the day to sing and talk and enjoy good company, up the pub they would go till closing time. Everyone used to go to the pub even if they made half a pint of beer last all night, because that's where you met your friends and chatted, had a singsong and had peas pudding and savaloys from the bar counter.

I was now old enough to go out to play on my own. The streets were our playground. There were horse and carts delivering goods to shops and coal to the houses, sometimes those who had skates would hang on to the backs of the horse and carts to get a free ride.
There were few cars and lorries to knock you down, if you did see a car it belonged to the doctor. We would play with marbles, skipping ropes and tops, which we would whip,

and all sorts of games with bats and balls and chasing. Our reading matter consisted of comics, some that I remember are Film Fun, Beano, Hotspur, Champion, Wizard and Rover. Each family would buy one then the rest would be swapped around. I do believe that I learnt to read more from those comics than any other way.

I don't remember much about my mum and dad (who was my stepfather) but I remember when I was little going to Southend-On-Sea for the weekend with them both. We arrived on Saturday and stayed in a house for the night. We had fish and chips and ice cream. I had never seen the sea and sand before and was enchanted with the whole lively scene, the funny hats and sticks of rock. My mum took off my dress and I went for a paddle in my knickers. I must have been about four. They had big boats taking people for a ride which had ropes hanging all around. I caught hold of the ropes and gradually worked my way to the front. Nobody saw me. There were a lot of people about laughing and splashing in the water.

I was pulled under the boat by the surge as it started out and was what they called keel hauled (pulled right under the bottom and out the other side). I would have drowned, someone must have saved me, but I don't remember much about it except to this day I will not go on a boat or ship or swim in the sea.

I remember one time we went hop picking. There was my Nan, Auntie Emmie, Auntie Florrie and about four children.

No men because the men had to go to work, the men were lucky if they got a week's holiday. We went for two weeks and lived in sheds with a shelf which we had to climb up on to sleep. The farmer would supply us with big cotton bags which we had to fill with hay to sleep on, no beds, we just lay those bags on the floor of the shelf and larked about until we fell asleep.

The roofs of the sheds were corrugated iron and when it rained it made a deafening sound which to me was comforting because I was dry inside. There was another shed outside which was used for cooking, almost the same as the one we slept in but it had no ends to it, just a roof and two sides. There was a big iron pot which was hung over a wood fire - just like the gypsies used to do - and my Nan and Auntie Emmie would make delicious meals. We would roast potatoes and apples on a stick in the flames underneath the pot. We would talk and sing and laugh, what an adventure. Mind you we had to work hard. Every morning, whilst the dew was still on the trees and the ground was damp, we would make our way to the hop fields where we would be allocated a bin then the hop puller would pull down the vines with a long pole and we had to pick the hops.
In those days, without any contraception, the wives had large families, sometimes one every year, so you can see for a working-class family money was very scarce.

My Nan always wore clothes down to her ankles and so did the other ladies. My Nan told me about Mrs Weekes who came hop picking with her brood of children. She was much poorer than us and couldn't afford the train fare for all her kids so when they got to the barrier at the railway station, she had two little ones get under her skirt, which was rather full, so that they would slip past without paying. With so many people and children pushing and shoving to get on the train no one noticed the funny way she was walking. We looked forward to the men coming at the weekend, they used to come in a lorry which was borrowed from the firm my uncle worked for. They used to trap rabbits for the pot and Saturday night they would all go to the village pub where they would have a grand sing song and walk home through the lanes singing.

It's strange but I can only remember not living with my Nan and Granddad three times when I was little. Once, we had a furnished room near Brixton market. It was around Christmas time. We had a lamb chop for dinner and my dad made me a blackboard and easel which I couldn't write on because it was painted with black paint and the chalk wouldn't write on it. It's funny how things stick in your mind. Whilst we were there in that one room, I found a threepenny bit on the way home from school. I always walked through the arcade in Brixton market. I liked to watch the people playing bingo for bags of groceries, 3d a go, so I had a go with the money I'd found and won a bag to take home. I could hardly carry it, there was so much there. My mum cried, we had bread and butter with strawberry jam for tea.

Another time I remember we had two rooms over a shop, I contracted Scarlet Fever, which was a killer in those days, and went into St Thomas's Hospital again, then went to convalesce in the country. I remember that place with its rows of beds in a big cold room with lots of beds and little children who cried for their mum - I expect I cried too. We used to sing grace before our meals: porridge in the morning, mince and potato for lunch and bread and jam for tea. When my mum came to get me from hospital, she had my favourite dinner waiting, rabbit stew with dumplings. I was so hungry and thin, I had been very ill and was lucky to have survived. She said I very nearly finished off the whole potfull.

Another time I remember living in a flat in Streatham. I used to wear a key around my neck to get in when I came home from school (Mum always had to work all her life - not for luxuries, just to survive). I would tidy up, peel the potatoes for dinner then sit and do my homework. I don't remember living there very long till one day I came home to find everything had gone, nothing left. Just imagine it, going home to your flat, opening the door to find no furniture, nothing in the kitchen, no clothes, just empty.

I sat on the floor and waited for Mum, frightened. Back we went to Nan's once again. We always went back, just mum and me. I found out later that my dad was a gambler and used to get into terrible debt with the bookies and ran away for months at a time to avoid being beaten up. He used to just turn up at Nan's, sometimes after three months, and mum would go off with him leaving me behind.

I don't think he was a gentleman's valet for very long and I don't really know what he did. I only know that mum always had to go out to work.

My Auntie Nin, who my real dad Bob married, lived in Bermondsey and they lived in a high block of flats, no lift. Everything had to be carried to the top floor where she lived. Nin had a boy at the same time as my mum had me, they called him Kenny. He used to work with his father at the docks.

One day he came home with a bad headache when he was about 17, a brick had fallen on his head (they never wore protective helmets in those days). My Auntie Nin came home from work - she was a cook - and found him dead in bed.

Nin had four more children, Bob, Rene, Stella and Allan. I used to stay with Auntie Nin in the summer holidays. I think she was a school cook at that time so had the same time off as the children.

I loved going around there, we played a lot in the yard downstairs. As I got a bit older, twelve to thirteen, we used to play kiss chase and run all around the balconies trying to dodge the boys. There was one boy I didn't try to dodge very hard and it was a thrill to have him give me a quick peck. I met him years later and he recognised me. I was about 50 years old then.

We lived in Robsart Street for some years which was about a mile from Brixton market.

I decided when I was about ten years old to try to earn some money so I took my cousin Albert, we always called him Albie, with me and the cart we pulled along, and after school went to the market and collected empty orange and apple boxes from under the stalls (the stall holders were glad to get rid of them). We would break them up by stamping on them so that we could carry a nice lot of wood, then we would take it home and I would chop it all up for firewood. Every day we would do this and on Saturday we loaded our cart and went knocking on doors selling firewood in an old tin bowl for 2d a bowl. We got so many orders for a sack full that we only went out on Saturday and afterwards delivered sackfulls, 2 shillings a sack. I did all the chopping because my cousin Albie wasn't old enough. He was only six so he filled the sacks with the chopped wood. My hands used to get sore with blisters and chapped with the cold. I saw my mum come home that first week. It was pouring with rain, she took her shoes off, they had big holes in the soles into which she was putting newspaper. I took a look at the size and made up my mind that the first week's money I collected would go to buying her new shoes. I'll never forget her face when I gave her the bag with the new shoes in.

The next week I bought myself the first pair of new shoes I'd ever had.

A wonderful thing happened about this time; the radio had come along. To make it go there was an accumulator filled with acid. We would sit round the radio listening to everything that came on. Mind you, Nan only had it on lunch time for the news and the evening for a few hours because it cost 2d to have the accumulator charged up once a week. One of the boys had to carry it to the oil shop, leave it there and bring another back in its place.

We moved to Clapham before I could make a fortune with the wood (you know I can hardly remember my stepfather; I don't know if he came or not). The school I went to was old and had big stone staircases with iron rails, everything was painted dark brown and dark green - not like the bright modern classrooms of today. I loved school, I was eager to learn and worked hard. There was a composition exam about safety which every school in England had to enter. Would you believe it, I won for my school and my mum had to take me to the Albert Hall in the heart of London, to collect my certificate. I must have been eleven years old then.
I was very light on my feet and my P.T. instructor used to have me out front to show the rest of the class how it was done. I was in the netball team. I had a teacher called Miss Laundry. She had iron grey hair twisted into a bun and was very strict. I was her favourite because I couldn't take my

own material for sewing class so I used to sew her undies for her - she taught me how to do the neatest stitches.

We had no one misbehaving in that school, if by chance anyone did, it was straight to the headmaster for '6 of the best'. The exams were coming to find who would go to grammar school. I desperately wanted to go and wear the uniform that the other grammar school children had. I was in the top group at school so if I worked hard there was no reason why I shouldn't pass. I did pass and ran home to tell Nan and Mum. I was so excited, imagine me going to grammar school, the only one in my family to do so. You don't think about the price of everything when you are eleven years old. The uniform, the books, even pens and pencils had to be supplied by your own parents. Mine couldn't, so I stayed where I was. What's the point of crying over something that can't be helped? - but I did. I cried myself to sleep and couldn't let anyone see that I cared. I had a consolation, however, I was made Head Girl of my school (by the way I've still got my badge) and it was my task to pick my own prefects.

We had a huge girl in my class who was feared by everyone except one or two who kept in with her, perhaps they were scared to do otherwise. Anyway, the day I was made Head Girl she was waiting outside the school and picked a fight with me. I had never had a fight or hit anyone in my life but I had to defend myself and even though I was half her size I managed to hurt her a little bit, not as much as she hurt me. Then a man came and broke us apart.

I gained that girl's respect and decided to make her a prefect. She was a marvelous prefect, nobody would misbehave on the stairs or anywhere else for that matter when she was there and, do you know, she changed from being a bully and even started to do better work in the classroom. I'll never forget Gladys, for that was her name.

Me Aged 17

We used to go to the pictures on Saturday morning for 2d, talking pictures had just come in, the cinema would be packed with noisy boys and girls eagerly awaiting the serial film which had left the heroine hanging from a cliff, or the cowboy about to be tortured by Indians, or some villain sneaking up behind the hero, when hundreds of children would shout - "Look behind you Mr!" It was so exciting to us youngsters who had never had much to look forward to, it was a thrill and we would act out the film we had seen all the week.

At that time our big sweet shop, I think it was called Meesons, would sell a quarter of sweets for a penny and give you another quarter free. I didn't buy sweets but my best friend would share hers with me and her two brothers. I would have loved to have gone to the pictures every week but I wasn't that lucky. My friend would act out with her brothers what they had seen so I wouldn't feel left out. I loved my friend, her dad had a grocer's shop and sometimes on the way home from school we would go in and have a glass of Corona, soft drink. My mum came home from work to find me upset. I had toothache. It was too late to take me to St. Thomas's hospital so she said "Put your coat on, I am going to take you out" and It was wonderful, Dorothy Lamour in the Jungle Princess. It cost my mum 9d, 6d for her and 3d for me. It is something I will never forget. It was all the money my mum had - she had to walk to work next day which was a Friday, pay day. That walk was about 4 miles.

Whilst we lived in Clapham there was a night when there was a great commotion. Everyone seemed to be out in the street, the sky was lit up with a crimson glow. The wonderful Crystal Palace was on fire. That wonderful building made of glass was burnt down in one night but to a little girl of ten it was very pretty and exciting.

CHAPTER 3
War Evacuation- I get My First Job -I Meet Reg

September 1939 was a terrible time for all children, war with Germany had begun. The kids had to be put in a safe place. We were called evacuees. We were given gas masks which I hated. I felt that I couldn't breathe with it on. You know, I can still smell the awful rubber when I think about it. My mum took me to school with my small bag of clothes, my gas mask and my name and school pinned to my coat and said goodbye.

The station was crowded, we had to keep together, nobody knew where we were going. My train went to Brighton and we were put in a school hall waiting for someone to come and claim us. The people in Brighton were told we were coming and told to come and take as many children as they could take care of.

The little ones were the first to go, then most of the bigger boys - they would be able to help on the farms. We had arrived in the morning, we had a sandwich and a cold drink but we were tired and frightened. We were in a strange place and didn't know anyone except our teacher. When was somebody coming to claim the rest of us? It was dark and still there were children left. No-one else arrived to take us, so a van was loaded and driven round the streets, knocking on doors trying to persuade people to take us in.

Then there were only three of us left. Our teacher knocked on the door of a small shop and, finding that the lady lived there alone, made her take us. She didn't want us and told the teacher so.

She took us upstairs to an empty room, no floor covering, no curtains, nothing at all. Our teacher said 'I'll soon sort this out for you' and 'you are obliged to do your bit like everyone else' - so our teacher went and got three camp beds and some bedding and we were billeted with this spinster lady who didn't want us. We went to bed with no food, in the dark and huddled together till we cried ourselves to sleep. It was winter.

We used to go to school for half a day because we had to share it with the children who lived in Brighton, the rest of the day we used to wander about, no lunch, until the lady would let us come in. She was a witch, she hated us and wanted us out. We had cornflakes for breakfast every day with milk, and our evening meal was corned beef with boiled potatoes and not much at that. Our mums would send us what little pocket money they could afford, and we would spend it on chips. We couldn't write home. We had no money for stamps and we were frightened to tell anyone in case there was trouble - we were all 13 years old. For months we lived like this, bitterly cold all through the winter, wandering about along the seafront in the wind and rain every afternoon, our folks never came to visit us. They couldn't afford the fare or get time off work.

32

Pat, my friend, fainted at school and was taken to the doctor. When he examined her, he found she was covered in boils and sores and was under weight and undernourished. She told him how we were living and all three of us were taken away and put in new homes. We were all in the same condition.

You know as I write this, I live that time over again, and think of other children that were in the same boat as my two friends and me, the tears are not very far away, and I feel very emotional. How lucky I was, I went to a loving family with a nice warm home, lots to eat and a nice comfy bed. I was treated like their own daughter, no more roaming the streets in the cold, straight home from school to a lovely tea, food that I had never had before. Their daughter and I used to put on shows with the help of her mum and dad. We would dress up in all sorts of costumes which they had used because they had both worked in the circus. They were midgets but their daughter was normal. This was a happy time even though I missed my family. My mum came and took me home back to London a week before my 14th birthday. We went back to Nan's. Nan's was always my home. I really didn't know my mother and father much at all but I was much loved and it was natural for me because that was how I was brought up. Auntie Emmie and her three boys were still there. I don't know if they were evacuated or not but it was nice to see them again. I used to look after them, take them up the park and kick a ball about, put them to bed and read them a story.

Mum

We were now living in Shakespeare Road, Brixton and it was time for me to stop being a child and get a job - in those days we started work at 14. Dad wasn't with us again, mum still worked full time but this time she worked at Vauxhall gas works. Women did men's jobs during the war and her job was to get inside big containers and clean them out. My mum had her picture in the papers showing women at war. She wasn't in a group, she was on her own seen with a shovel loading a wheelbarrow.

On my birthday, unbeknown to my folks, I decided to go after a job. I had seen a notice in the Post Office window for a counter clerk just around the corner from where we lived, so I went in and applied. The man gave me a form to fill in with simple arithmetic on it i.e. if someone wanted a postal order for 2 shillings and had to pay 3d duty and gave you a pound, how much change would you give them? There were four sheets of paper to fill out which I found so easy. I was always good at maths, especially mental arithmetic. I handed it to the man who had been timing me. He said "have you done it already?", then checked it and found it all correct. I didn't get the job though because I was only fourteen and you had to be sixteen to work in a Post Office. He said he was sorry and would love to have me, just a minute though, his sister wanted a junior in her office in the Strand, "Hold on I'll phone her" he said and a few minutes later he gave me instructions where to go. I told the nice man that I didn't have any money for my fare so he gave me 4d which was enough for my return fare. I got the job and began work with his sister.

She had a name like a flower, Miss Narcissus. It was an Auctioneers, Surveyors and Valuers office. I earned 12/6d per week. I had to give 10 shillings a week to my mum for my keep and had 2/6d for myself. Out of the 2/6d I had to buy my own clothes, shoes and anything else I wanted. I stayed there till I was sixteen. I had to light the boss's fire in the morning, which I hated, then I had to write lots of envelopes by hand, run errands, go to the Post Office and all the usual jobs of a junior. I taught myself to type and work a switchboard, work a filing system - in those days there weren't all the complicated things like photocopiers and computers and if you wanted to balance your books which were in pounds, shillings and pence, halfpennies and farthings, written like "£ s d", you had to do it in your head, so I gained a bit of knowledge about books and book-keeping because I was good at figures and liked to do it.

I left for another job when I was sixteen because I felt I couldn't go any further, it was only a small business with about fifteen staff. The lure of the cinema had caught me, so I got a job at the J Arthur Rank offices in Wardour Street right in the heart of the city. I think I was earning about three pounds a week by then.

Let me go back to when I was fourteen. I had made new friends after a while, and we made up a sort of a club - there were ten of us boys and girls. I don't remember where my bike came from but we used to go out for rides on Sundays and sometimes we took a picnic and stayed out all day. Most times we went to Shirley Hills because we liked to see the aeroplanes at Croydon Airport on the way. Our church hall used to have dances on Saturday night, and we all used to go - that's where we learned how to dance.

We five girls all had a boy for a partner but we didn't pair off into twos, we were just all friends together. The boys always took us home, a different boy each Saturday. I had to be home by 10 o'clock and one Saturday I was having such a good time - I loved dancing - I didn't notice the time, so I didn't get home till 11 o'clock. Remember, there was a war on, there were guns firing, bombs dropping and in fact all hell was breaking loose - we didn't all go to the shelters every time there was an air raid, else we wouldn't have any life worth living. My mother opened the door for me and screamed and beat me all the way up the stairs with a stick. She thought that when I didn't get home on time that I was dead and was so worried she didn't know what she was doing. That was the only time in my life that I was physically punished - but she did cuddle me and was sorry and crying for what she had done. I was never late home again.

One of our boys was called Dennis, he and his sister were both in our group. I loved Dennis with all my heart - my first love. He was a wonderful dancer and all the girls loved to dance with him. I'd never ever kissed him but my heart would go bang, bang, whenever I saw him. I was fourteen, he was sixteen. You know I never ever forgot that boy even to this day when I have been married to my true love for nearly 50 years. I still have his picture in my album. More about Dennis later.

We were now living in a big house with a baker's downstairs. There was my Nan, granddad, Auntie Emmie and three boys Albie, Ronnie and Teddy, there was my

Auntie Florrie and my mum and dad and me Margaret. We were still in the Brixton area, this time in Railton Road.

My Auntie Flo used to serve in the bakery, sometimes I would give her a hand on Saturday. Although we had big ovens downstairs where the bread and cakes used to be made, these were not in use, the produce came from a master baker who delivered daily.

Our cellar was reinforced, we had big strong poles to hold up corrugated sheets on the ceiling and every night we would sleep in our cellar. Sometimes when the air raids got really bad, neighbours would come down with us.

One night we lost our home. The Germans had started dropping land mines. Land mines would not just make a small hole, they would demolish whole streets and the blast would demolish adjoining streets. Our house just collapsed on top of us, fortunately we were safe in our reinforced cellar.

Looking back to that time, I can't remember feeling afraid, although the noise of bombs dropping, and Ack Ack guns blazing away was enough to frighten anybody. We were all alive and would soon be dug out from what was once our home.

We were given a house in Perran Road, Tulse Hill. It had been hit by an oil bomb and was a bit of a mess, but beggars couldn't be choosers, it was a roof over our heads.

People we didn't know helped us out with bits and pieces and we soon settled in - we still had that awful outside toilet with cut up newspaper hanging on a string. There was a bathroom but no heater for hot water, so we never used it. I started going to a church hall called The Brotherhood. I was fifteen years old. It wasn't very special but it was cheap and the band we had was quite good. All of our boy friends had gone into the forces, so often most of the dancers were girls. We had to dance together, that's where I learned how to take the lead. It was wonderful when the lads came home on leave, they always came dancing and then we really enjoyed ourselves.

One night there were my two friends and me walking home from the dance, there was a terrible air raid going on, guns blazing and incendiaries dropping, the sky was lit up by fires, then we arrived at the bottom of Gypsy Hill where my friend Joyce lived. By this time, we were running, her house was gone, together with her mum and dad and brother. Things like this were an everyday occurrence.

There were no buses running at night. If you went out to the pictures, or dancing, you had to walk home after about 10 o'clock. When there was no moon it was pitch black, there were no lights anywhere. In fact, if you lit a cigarette up, somebody would shout at you, not that I was smoking at that time. The air raid wardens would knock on doors if they saw a chink of light showing.

One night my friend Rose (she has been my friend since I was sixteen and we went everywhere together) and I went to a firemen's party at Peckham. It was in the fire station itself and we had a lovely time until the air raid started and the firemen were all called out to fight the fires.

Rose and I had to walk home, it was about 4 miles. We were supposed to be taken home but all the firemen were out and the girls were forgotten. We walked through a terrible air raid, bombs falling, Ack-Ack guns blazing, planes fighting. When the fighting was overhead, we ducked into doorways to avoid the falling shrapnel - when I look back, I marvel how we took all these things for granted. We were half running and walking when we got breathless. There was no moon that night and the only light came from the fires which lit up the sky. The fight came towards us and we could hear the shrapnel falling all around us (if a piece of that hit you, you didn't stand a chance). We were really scared by this time, so knocked on a house and asked the lady to give us shelter. She very kindly let us sleep on her sofa and gave us a drink of cocoa.

Next morning, we made our way home and, what do you know, we were only a five minute walk away from my house, but we didn't know that in the dark.

I would rather go dancing than do anything else. I was always light on my feet and could follow any partner easily. We used to have a dancing competition every Saturday night and no matter who my partner was we usually won.

The prize was a pair of nylons for the girls and cigarettes for the boys. I never lacked a partner and I used to dance every dance. Some of the girls were a bit fed up that I kept winning the stockings. You just could not get nylon stockings, even if you had the coupons to do so, so they complained to the manager.

I was asked not to take part in any of the competitions to keep the rest of the girls happy, and I was told that I would never have to pay to come in. I loved to enter the competitions, but I agreed, after all I would be saving money.

A week before Christmas I met a boy who wanted to take me to the dance on Boxing day. His name was Charlie Brown, so I thought why not? He was waiting to be called up for the Air Force, he was in the Air Training Corp. As usual we went to the Brotherhood, our local dance. I was just sixteen and it was the first time that I had ever gone out alone with a boy.

When we arrived, he introduced me to some of his friends, among them was a tall, slim young man called Reg. I had a dance with Reg and when the interval came all the boys went over to the pub opposite to have a drink. Reg didn't go and stayed behind talking to me. I never went to pubs, I was just sixteen. Reg said "Shall we go outside to get some air?", which we did and almost immediately he put his arms around me and gave me a big kiss - my first kiss - it shook me, the force of it, I was tingling right down to my toes, and I was a little afraid of my feelings. "We had better go back in" I said, and I hurried back inside.

Reg 18

Reg carried on dancing with me the rest of the evening and asked to take me home (I don't remember what happened to Charlie Brown). I thought that Reg was rather nice with his thick dark wavy hair and nice smile, so I agreed. I only lived about half an hour's walk away, still living with my Nan, and when we arrived, he kissed me goodnight and made a date to take me to the cinema the next night.

That night he had to walk about five miles home because he and his mum and dad were staying the night at his Auntie's house and do you know it turned out that he only lived five minutes away from me. I wasn't exactly walking on air at meeting him. I was too young to be involved with anything serious, anyway I was still in love with Dennis who I met on the odd occasion when he came home on leave, never with him alone, always with the rest of the gang sometimes at his house, sometimes at the dance.

I had all my time taken up with Reg now, he was really very nice and I liked him a lot. He was an apprentice in the printing trade so didn't have much money. Very proud was Reg and he would never let me pay for anything when we went out, so we used to go for walks or sometimes I would watch him play football.

He loved football and was a boxer and he was a terrific runner. He had a medal for running at Crystal Palace and no one could beat him at school. He was very fit playing football which he played right up to joining the Air Force.

Reg 20

Reg wanted to be a pilot and was very disappointed to fail the eye test. He had whooping cough as a little toddler and his eye went into the corner. He had to wear glasses for a time to straighten his eyes and didn't realise there was anything wrong as he never wore glasses afterwards. He was made a Navigator, but I know he was bitterly disappointed.

I didn't want him to go away and when he did, I missed him and realised I loved him. The war was on, would I ever see him again? His mum and dad made me most welcome and I used to see them a lot. When Reg went into the Air Force his home became my second home and I got to know all his family. Reg only had one sister Doris but he had loads of uncles and aunts.

For a time, I worked with his mum and sister in a canteen at Victoria Station. His mother was a very kindly person who was the manageress and everyone called her "mum" and she was greatly respected. The servicemen used to come in for a cup of tea and a snack in between trains.
When a train load of men arrived, it was all systems go, a mad rush to serve hundreds of men in a short time.

I was sent to work in a 'munitions' factory in West Norwood. It was a huge place backing onto Norwood cemetery. I was in the office as a typist. I used to type stencils which I would run off on a machine then I had to deliver them around the factory.

Walking round the factory delivering these orders was a nightmare for me, because I used to get wolf whistles, and asked out for a date by many of the young men, and old ones too. I hurried up as fast as I could to get back to my own office.

One time there was a bug going around. They say it came off the money brought in by the soldiers from abroad. The whole factory had to go to a cleansing station, even if you hadn't caught the bug yet. You certainly knew if you had caught the bug, it used to burrow under your skin and breed at a very fast rate. It made you itch like mad.

The government had set up these cleansing stations and we were collected in coaches and taken there about 50 at a time. We had a bath, then the lady came to paint us. She came, a huge buxom woman with a bucket of evil smelling pink gunge and a whitewash brush - just imagine us standing against the wall with this woman slapping us up and down with this big whitewash brush, first the back then the front, we had to sit on a stool until it had dried on us. It still reminds me of the old song that my Nan and granddad used to join in and sing at their parties.

"I painted her, I painted her,
up the alley and down the back,
in every hole, every crack,
I painted her down the Drury Lane,
I painted her old tomato over and over again"

I had to put that bit in because, when we were all driven back to work, we fell about laughing and forgot all about being shy. It's a good job it was women only and not mixed.

Every morning going to work we had a long walk past the cemetery. One morning I left for work during an air raid. We tried to carry on in the air raids because they came so often that if we didn't carry on, no work would be done and that's no way to win a war.

Whilst we were walking, a Doodle Bug came over - those Doodle Bugs were very noisy and came in very low over our heads. When the engine cut out, we knew the bomb would drop and we should take cover. The only place we could go was to lie down against the houses on one side of the road - remember the cemetery was on the other side. The Doodle Bomb dropped in the next street shattering all the glass windows which came at you like sharp knives. Fortunately, we were protected by the walls of the houses, but we could hear the houses falling down, and taste the dust as it rose in the air.

We carried on going to work, there were hundreds of us that side of the houses. If the bomb had dropped our side, a lot of us would have died, but that is the luck of the war, if your name is on it, you will get it.

The only holiday that I had ever had was one weekend at Southend-on-Sea when I was a toddler so when there was a notice put on the bulletin board at work asking for volunteers to go to work on the farms for a week, two friends and I decided to go in our week's holiday. Pat, Rose and I used to go out as a threesome, so there we were sleeping in a tent and washing in cold water in a makeshift wash house and eating in a barn.

It was in Oxford and everything was arranged for us. We had to work in the mornings but had the afternoons off. We received no pay but had all our food and transport paid for. The weather was glorious and we three had a wonderful time. No air raids, no bombs, no fires. It was as if there was no war on. I would have liked to stay there till the war was over.

I came back quite plump, even with the hard work we had to do (stacking corn) and clearing the land.

The food we had - as much as we liked - eggs, bacon, meat, cream, butter, creamy milk, fresh veg, home-made bread and scones. For girls who had never known much else except rationing it was like Shangri La.

We swam and walked and sunbathed and laughed a lot until it was time to go home.

Reg would come home as often as possible on leave for weekends and sometimes the odd day and we would enjoy each other's company. When I say that we would enjoy each other's company, I mean we clung together, hugged and kissed, we couldn't bear not to be near each other. His mother said that we broke the springs in the sofa, but we never did go the whole way.

At this time, he was doing his training and I was beginning to realise that we were meant for each other. I knew that Reg loved me and it gave me a warm feeling to be with him, to feel his arms around me was sheer delight. There was a war on, people were being killed all the time. Reg

48

was about to join the fight which was a very dangerous one. We were both too young to make an official commitment, so we poured out our love in our letters to each other three or four times a week.

When Reg had to go abroad, I spent more and more time with his mum and dad. I used to call in on my way home from work to light their fire and tidy up a bit. It could be bitterly cold with no central heating and only a fire in one room, so I know that they appreciated to come home to some warmth.

Reg's sister Dol had a son, his name was Laurie. He was a border at a private school, ten minutes away. His Grandma and Grandad had him home for the weekend, so at weekends I used to take him up the park, or to the pictures, or we would just play indoors.

My father was living with us now at Nan's. It was only a small house so we, my mother, father and myself had one bedroom and one kitchen. This was a very bad time for my mum, you see my father had a stroke and was paralysed all down one side.

There was no free medicine. When I think back at what it was like to be ill in those days, I thank God that we have National Health today.

My mum had to find the money for doctor's fees, medicine, treatment, everything. She couldn't go to work because dad needed constant looking after so money was scarce. Thank the Lord for my Nan, she was always there and would help anyone.

My father was paralysed for two years and was bedridden. When he was able to walk it was with great difficulty with two sticks. I wonder how quickly he would have got better if he had had hospital treatment and physiotherapy. As it was, he was home all the time and didn't have any hospital care at all.

I really wanted to do more to help so I went to King's College Hospital on Denmark Hill, after work, to do voluntary work. I would go as often as I could and worked extremely hard.
At first, I would do bedpans, then bedmaking, then the food trolley. Always the tidying up before the doctors' rounds.

I progressed to changing dressings, taking blood pressure and temperatures. The beds were so close together because we had to make room for more and more people who had been injured. It was a terrible time, the injuries people received were unmentionable.
One night the air raid siren went off, we were busy pushing beds down to the lower floors for safety, we did this every night. I was working on one of the upper floors and most of the beds had been moved when I heard the Doodle Bug. I stopped and listened hoping that the engine wouldn't cut out. It did, I lay on the young man who's bed I was just going to move and waited the few seconds for the bomb to

drop. When it did the blast shattered all the windows, the shards of glass where sticking into the wall on the other side of the ward, we were lucky to still be alive because there was glass all around us. The nurses as always worked very hard, they never complained although the hours were long and arduous.

The air raids were getting worse and many times I had narrow escapes from being injured or killed. At last everything got too much for me. I was burning the candle at both ends, in other words I was working too hard with little sleep, also with the constant bombardment we were being subjected to. I had a nervous breakdown.

It happened this way, I was coming home on a bus from Brixton where I had been shopping, when we were in collision with another bus which was swerving to avoid a hole in the road. I was thrown from the back of the bus to the front because I was standing up at the time. I was knocked out and taken to hospital. When I recovered, they took me home where I stayed for the next three months. I couldn't go to work so I had to see the firm's doctors who announced that I was having a nervous breakdown. I didn't go mad, it's just that I couldn't co-ordinate my body to do the things it should do.

It was strange trying to walk up and down stairs or even to walk on a level without falling. Trying to eat was most difficult, it was a job to find my mouth even with a spoon. Now I know what it's like to be a baby and have to learn all over again how to do the easiest things. It's a good job that I could still think for myself. I must say the factory I worked for were very decent, the sister in charge of the medical center, came to see me every week bringing my wages.

Dreadful things happened during the bombardment of London. I remember one day I was visiting my other grandmother who lived near the Oval cricket ground, when there was a fight above us with our planes shooting down a Jerry. He bailed out and his parachute caught up on the top of the high wall which was covered in barbed wire around the cricket ground. I ran to see together with crowds of other people who had watched the whole thing. They ran with weapons like frying pans, saucepans, brooms, anything they could lay their hands on, here was someone who they could vent their anger on. They couldn't reach him. He was high up but he must have been terrified to see this howling mob of people waiting to kill him (I was frightened out of my skin). The police came with a van and got him down into the van but the people were not going to have that, they turned the van over and at this point I ran away and didn't want to see any more. These kindly people who I believed wouldn't hurt a soul, mostly women and old men, had something to have made them behave in this manner because shortly before the incident there had been a very bad air raid and bombs had been dropped on Kennington Park which is just by the Oval cricket ground. The bombs made a direct hit on a huge air raid shelter containing hundreds of people all of whom were killed. So, you can understand if a lot of your loved ones had been blown to pieces, you might well have behaved the same way.

I believe that it was easier for the children to have lived in London during the war because they didn't know anything else, they were brought up to that way of life.

Rationing, queuing- up was left to the mothers to worry about. Not all the children were evacuated and some who were, came home again. Some stayed until they were old enough to go to work and some never came home again. They stayed with their foster parents because either their folk had been killed or they preferred to stay where they were.

You know we didn't have to be hungry in the war. You would always get offal that wasn't rationed. I remember with fondness the great rabbit stew with dumplings, rabbit pie and baked rabbit, stuffed hearts, liver and onions etc.

Dairy produce was rationed, eggs, cheese, milk and butter were very, very difficult. One egg now and again, no milk to drink just enough for a few cups of tea, cheese - well not really enough to make a decent sandwich. I remember Reg came home on a week's leave with his ration card. His mum sent him to the grocers to get his dues and he came home with them in one pocket.

Chickens were not very plentiful. We only had chickens a few times a year. When I think of all the food that is available today, huge supermarkets and people coming out loaded up with all the good things that they supply.

Most of Nan's children were married and away now except for Auntie Emmie who would always be around, mum and dad and granddad and me. Granddad was retired now. He used to spend his days walking our dog which was a Dalmation with hundreds of spots (named 'Trouble' because she kept having puppies), or sitting on the wall outside our house talking to passers-by. In the evenings, he would sometimes take Nan to the pub which was just over the road, to have a Guinness. I never ever knew my Nan or granddad to be ill and they never ever had a row, not that I know of anyway.

One day there was a knock on the door, and there stood Fred's officer. He had come to tell us that Fred, Nan's youngest, had been killed on D Day during the invasion. He was in a tank which was blown up. It was on his twenty first birthday.

My uncle Fred was the one who I used to follow to school when I was three years old. I loved him like my big brother. He used to call me Laz because when I was small, I got hold of a tin of Lazenbie's loganberries which had been opened as a treat for Sunday tea and I ate the lot, covering myself in red juice all over.

Fred used to take me to the Locarno dancing when he came home on leave. He was a very quiet man and I missed him a lot. Fred was the only member of our family to be killed during the war so I suppose we were lucky. Some of my friends lost all of their family.

My dad was able to move about a bit now, so my mum went back to work. She got a job as a cook in a pub, nothing special, just plain home cooking - so I could keep a bit more of my wages to save up for - who knows - a wedding. Surely the war would be over soon.

We had Vera Lynn, Ann Shelton, all the big bands and my favourite Glen Miller to listen to on the radio. I still loved to dance, and my friend Rose and I always went together. Rose had yet to meet her love and I was content to wait for Reg although it was nice to go dancing and meet the boys when they came home on leave, especially Dennis.

Rose and I used to go to the pictures every week. It was only a shilling or one and six (7 1/2p today) to go in but we had to queue for ages and sometimes even when we got in, we had to stand. One night we went to Brixton to see 'Gone With The Wind'. The picture was four hours long and whilst we were in there, there was an air raid and a bomb dropped right in the entrance of our cinema. The film was stopped and the manager told us that we couldn't leave because there was an unexploded bomb outside and we had to stay until it was dismantled.

We watched that film all night, some people lay on the floor and tried to get some sleep - how could they sleep with a huge unexploded bomb just outside the door? It was daylight when we were allowed to leave, what a relief.

Lots of people used to go to the pubs for their enjoyment but people like Rose and I would prefer to go to the cinema or better still dancing. Reg was overseas. He was away for a year and through our letters to each other we became more and more in love. I was growing up and knew that we would always be together if God willing and we both survived the war. Would this war ever end? Everyone was tired and although we put on a brave face, we never knew what the next day would bring.

Living in London during the war was the most dangerous place to be. I was working in the Strand in the heart of London at one time. We had terrible air raids, a lot of the roads had great holes in with burst water mains, and gas pipes. Everyone tried to get to work, the buses were still running but not on their usual run, they had to make lots of detours around the side streets trying to find a way to get through to their destination. You can imagine the sights we saw on the way, houses collapsed, water spurting out of the broken water pipes, ordinary people digging in the rubble from the houses looking for people who were buried. This was an everyday occurrence.

Lorries would come along and stop at the bus stops telling the people where they were trying to get to, they would help them to get up onto the back of the lorry, never asking for any fare, but had a tin can tied up so that you could drop a coin in. These lorries were a blessing for we all wanted to get to work.

There is a famous place in London where the Bank of England is, in fact the underground station which runs underneath is called The Bank. There was a bomb dropped right on top of the station, a great hole in the middle of the road. The army built a pontoon bridge over the hole so that the buses could still use the road. As you went over it you could look down and see the train lines, it was very wobbly going over the bridge and the bus seemed to sway from side to side.

I was staying with my Auntie Nin who lived in the Borough, which is close to the River Thames. We slept in the air raid shelter at night which had been built in between the high-rise flats. There was one of these air raid shelters in every other block. This particular night had been very bad, all the docks were alight, the firemen were out in force, fire-fighters from other towns had been called in to help control the fires, it was the worst night of the war in my opinion.

When we left our shelter in the morning, all you could smell was the smoke, and the dust. The shelter in the next block to ours had been hit, people were tearing at the rubble searching for bodies with their bare hands.

My auntie made us come away, but not until I had seen an ear lying in the grass. I didn't say anything, I just picked up a dustbin lid which was lying nearby and put it over the ear.

My memories of it would fill a book so I shall get on with my own story. My friend Rose met an American soldier at our local dance, the Brotherhood, just before the end of the war. Then it seemed all of a sudden it was all over, everyone was dancing and singing.

We made up a foursome with Rose, Al and his friend and me and we went to Trafalgar Square to join in the celebrations. I have never seen so many people in one place in my life. Everyone was hugging and kissing each other. This was V.E. day, victory in Europe, May 1945, the beginning of the end of the war.

We danced in the streets, we did knees- up, people jumped in the fountains, policemen gave us their helmets to wear and joined in the fun. Reg was on his way home, please God he wouldn't be bombed or torpedoed now that it was nearly over.

No news from Reg for weeks, then everything happened at once. The war in Europe was over. I was having a perm, preparing myself for Reg's homecoming. Waiting at the bus stop I saw a taxi with one of Reg's uncles driving (quite a few of his uncles were taxi drivers). There was a kit bag beside him and somehow I knew that Reg was in there on his way home. I felt like running after the cab, I was so excited.

I got off the bus and went straight round to his house and rang the bell - Reg answered the door and we fell into each other's arms, hugging and kissing. We had made it, we had both come through the war alive and well. All the relatives congregated around Reg's house. His mum was looked upon as the head of the family. A lot of them had lived with her and Dad throughout the war because of time bombs and being bombed out.

The Japanese surrendered in August (VJ Day) and we all piled into cars and taxis and headed for Carshalton to meet up with more relatives in their local pub. There were fires in the streets, people celebrating, dancing, waving at us shouting good wishes.

I remembered the time when Reg was home on a week-end pass. We went dancing at the Brotherhood as usual, lots of his friends were there and he wanted me to go with him to the pub over the road in the interval. I wish I had never gone. Reg had just got me a lemonade shandy when the police came in, they were checking everyone's identity cards. I wasn't quite eighteen years old, so I wasn't allowed to be in a public house at all. They took all our particulars, I was scared stiff, I hadn't even sipped the shandy. Worse was to come, the next day a police car pulled up outside my house, two policemen had words with my Nan who had never been so ashamed in her life. What could I say, only that I was sorry. Reg got the worst of it though, he had to appear before his C.O. who gave him a right good talking to, taking young girls out to pubs etc, etc.

After all the street parties, things were going to get back to normal, but not for a long time. There would still be shortages of most things, food and clothes were still rationed, Dockets were needed for furniture, petrol was unobtainable but there was light, no more blackouts, no more wardens shouting 'douse that light' but, best of all, no more air raids.

Margaret 18

The great work of rebuilding would soon begin, jobs for everyone. In fact, there were not enough people to do all the work required so we recruited Jamaicans, Nigerians and almost anyone who wanted to come to our dear England. How we love our country, we would never live anywhere else!

A holiday camp had just come on the scene, called Maddisons. Reg's mum decided we should go on holiday there. His dad didn't want to go to any camp, he had enough of camps when he was in the army in the first world war, but with a lot of persuasion we went, Reg and me, Laurie, Dol's son, and Reg's mum and dad.

Reg's Mum, Dad, Nephew with Reg and me
at holiday camp just after the war

The chalets were quite primitive in those days but comfortable enough. There was a dining hall, a dance hall, play room with table tennis, children's playroom and a little way away a bar with slot machines. From now I will always call Reg's mum and dad "mum and dad" because that's what they were to me.

The food was absolutely fantastic. Breakfast was cereals, eggs and bacon, toast and marmalade or you could have kippers, haddock, boiled eggs, almost anything you wanted and as much as you could eat. Lunch was a full meal and enough to satisfy anyone. Dinner was the high spot of the day, three courses. We had turkey, chickens, roast beef, roast lamb, baked potatoes, plenty of fruit and veg. Mr Maddison, the owner, said we could have whatever we wanted so long as nothing was wasted. After all the skimping and saving and making do all through the war nobody was going to waste a thing.

Dad loved to go to the bar every night after dinner. The first night we went there was a piano on a small platform in the corner of the bar. (Dad loved to play, he could play almost any instrument). Mum said "Come on Ted, give us a tune", so that is exactly what he did. He played almost non- stop for 2 hours, with me prompting the next song. He couldn't read music but dad didn't need any. I just hummed a few bars and he knew it. The bar rang with music, everyone was singing and having a wonderful time, the piano was lined up with dad's favourite tipple, Guinness.

Everyone wanted to keep him playing and kept supplying him with his drink till closing time when we all went over to the dance hall for the rest of the evening.

The dance hall was almost empty every night 'till dad stopped playing when everyone went to the dance hall - for this became the regular thing. Dad was hoisted onto the piano every night and played his heart out - he loved it and they all loved him. The last night he was cheered "Good old Pop". That was his name, "Pop", all the week. Mum and dad came with us on holiday to chaperon us. They lived in the family chalets one side of the camp, Reg and I lived in the single chalets the other side of the camp, next door to each other. We had lots of kisses and cuddles and thinking back we certainly took chances with our emotions but nothing happened that we could be ashamed of, although many times we were tempted. It's a good job we weren't hard drinkers, otherwise we could easily have given in, loving each other as we did and still do. What a difference today, I still think that as far as love and marriage goes, it's still better to wait to be wed, there certainly wouldn't be so many divorces or children who don't know who their fathers are.

Reg and I on Holiday

CHAPTER 4
War Ends - We Marry

Time went by, Reg and I bought our engagement ring and decided with his mum's help that we couldn't wait to get married. We decided that now I was 20 years old and we had been together for 4 years, not living together which is the done thing these days, but together in a loving sense and both of us still virgins.

We chose the 28th June and all arrangements went ahead towards that day. Reg's mum, bless her, arranged everything. I was still living just across the road with Nan and granddad, Auntie Emmie and the three boys who were my cousins, my mum and dad and me. I was 20 years old and still sleeping in the same room as mum and dad. It was only a small house and no room for me anywhere else.

My dad hadn't been to work since as long as I could remember, he was walking with two sticks now after his stroke, and he was going to give me away in church. My sister-in-law, Dol, lent me her wedding dress and someone else in Reg's family gave me some material for two bridesmaid's dresses. We even had Reg's sister's son, Laurie, as a pageboy. I got married from Reg's mum and dad's house so he had to spend the night around his friend Les's home and would be at the church on our wedding day.

I've never seen so many people who came to the house before going to church and because it took so long to get rid of them my Dad and I were late leaving and it was raining. Uncle Jim held the umbrella over me as I arrived at the church. It was a lovely ceremony. I remember when we were kneeling at the altar being blessed that the sun came out and shone through the beautiful stained-glass window right on us.

Reg and I just Married

Coming out of the church I was kissed by a chimney sweep, dressed in his gear with his brushes over his shoulder - it was supposed to be lucky. Mum thought of everything. Reg's mum organised and paid for everything, flowers, photographer, band, MC, wedding cake.

I found out years later that the hall had been flooded the day before our wedding, and Mum had got all the family and friends in to clean up the mess. She hired a hall behind West Norwood Church for the reception. We had a three course meal with wine and eighty guests. I really was overcome that she had done so much. She was still a working woman, didn't own her own house, didn't have a car, didn't have any of the luxuries that we are used to today. She used her savings to give us a good start in life and I loved her. My mum and dad had nothing, so the little bit of savings I had went towards my mum's outfit and a suit for dad and a trousseau to take on honeymoon. We had a wonderful time at the party.

Just before the end, who should walk in? Dennis, the boy who I fell in love with when I was 14. He was in his sailor's uniform. I don't know how he knew I was getting married that day, I suppose one of our mutual friends told him. He came to me and wished me all the luck in the world and asked to have a last dance with me, which I did. Then he said 'goodbye', saying 'I wish it was me'. I never saw him again but I did hear that when he came out of the Navy he joined the police force just like his dad and when he answered an alarm in a factory a safe blew up just as he entered the room, which left him stone deaf.

Another time some years later I heard that he was married with three children. What a pity, a young man with all that rhythm in his dancing and his love of music, could become deaf so young - I wonder where he is now?

Getting back to our wedding day. Lots of people came back to mum's house to carry on with the party. We were going to live with mum and dad until we could find a place of our own and she had prepared Reg's room for us beautifully to spend our very first night together. Our bedroom was right next door to the front room where the party was. There was dad on the piano and there must have been at least 30 people around.

We couldn't go to bed so we drifted upstairs to have a chat and a cup of tea with Reg's sister Dol and Arthur, his brother-in-law (they lived on the next floor). At three o'clock in the morning, all was quiet so we crept downstairs to go to bed. After all the excitement of the day we were dead tired. We opened the door to our bedroom and there were two huge bodies in our bed snoring their heads off. We ended up on the floor in the front room surrounded by half eaten sandwiches and empty cups and glasses. Our wedding, what a disaster to end a perfect day.

We were going to Hastings for our honeymoon which we had booked up months before in a small hotel. A week before we were due to go we had a letter saying the hotel was closed due to change of ownership and the place was being redecorated.

The owners had arranged for us to go to a guest house nearby because they knew we were a honeymoon couple and didn't want us to lose our holiday. So that's where we went, ration books and all. They were a Scottish couple and we were so lucky. They gave us the best room next door to a lovely bathroom. We couldn't have been more looked after, biscuits and tea in bed in the morning, a good English breakfast (where did she get all the eggs and bacon?), plenty of food and sunshine to brighten our days. In the evenings we went out for a walk or to the cinema and came home and sat with our hosts in the kitchen drinking cocoa or having snacks. This was living which I had never had in my life and all too soon we were heading back to London and work.

CHAPTER 5
First Years of Marriage, Both Working to Secure Our Future

Our married life began by living with Reg's mum and dad. I was working at Smithfield market in the office of the transport manager. I travelled to work by train every day and things were working out fine. Reg went back to work as a compositor in the printing trade. He was put into print by his father who had worked all his life in the printing profession. Reg had to finish his apprenticeship when he came out of the air force, so he had to finish that before he could begin to earn decent money.

We decided that we wouldn't start a family until we got on our feet and had our own place, but in those days making decisions like that were taken out of our hands and we had no proper counselling on birth control. We were like innocent babes, our parents never told us anything, and we didn't learn anything at school either.

I became pregnant after two months of marriage. We immediately put our name down for a council flat but were told we had no hope until the baby was born and even then it was very unlikely that we would get anything with only one child.

There was such a terrible shortage of places to live after the war, what with all the destruction by the bombing - great gaps and holes in most streets, factories, blocks of flats, whole blocks of houses, shops destroyed, there was a lot of work to be done to get things back to normal. For some families things would never get back to normal because their loved ones had been killed or wounded.

Before the war it was easy to move, most people lived in rented accommodation, people didn't earn enough money to buy their own house and the people who could afford to own them very often would let a flat to pay the mortgage.

My Nan and Granddad would rent a house and only move when they couldn't afford to pay the rent, and move into a cheaper place, but that was before the war. I carried on working for about six months then I developed abscesses in a private place which grew to the size of an egg and stopped me from being able to work. I was sent to hospital but had to wait until they were ripe so they could be burst. I packed up work and went into hospital for a few days to have the job done.

Three times these dreadful things came back, always in the same place and each time I had to go back into hospital to have them burst. I was in terrible pain and unable to walk each time and mum couldn't understand why I was so distressed, after all she couldn't see anything. Then one day, when I was due to go back into hospital to have the last one burst, she came into my bedroom and asked to see it. When

71

I showed it to her, with much embarrassment, she cried and took me in her arms and hugged me.

Next day I went into hospital due to have the op in the morning. I was now seven months pregnant. During the night I was screaming with pain. The nurse gave me two aspirins which were absolutely useless and told me to be quiet because I was upsetting the rest of the ward. In the early hours of the morning I fell asleep exhausted with the pain, the thing had burst on its own and I was torn and bleeding. They rushed me to surgery and had to cut the whole thing away so that it could heal before my baby was born.

Reg had been pestering the housing people to give us a flat, he had even written to our M.P. who wrote to them asking if there was anything that they could do for us, especially as I was having such a bad time with my pregnancy.

Reg got a call from the housing manager to go and see him. It was the first time he had been able to get in to see him, this housing manger was too busy to see anyone before this. He really had a go at Reg for writing to the M.P. He said he hadn't anything to offer him but one place, and if he turned that down there was nothing else.

He was given an address on Brixton Hill, and Reg and I went to see it on the Saturday morning.
What a shock we had when we arrived there, some people were moving in, they had been given the flat the same time

as Reg which was only a few days before. Reg phoned the housing people on the following Monday, and wanted to know what they were playing at, nobody knew anything about it.

We got a flat just after this, what a flat, it was supposed to be temporary, our name was down for a new flat that was being built, so we decided to take it and make a start. Our flat was made out of a residential school. It had been split into two to make two houses and each house was divided into three flats. We had the top flat which had been a dormitory. There were five big windows in the living room and they had partitioned it off to make a small kitchen and bedroom. The kitchen had a gas stove inside the door, next to it was a bath with a lid on it, then the door into the living room, there was a window, then on the other wall was a small sink with a single draining board and an Ascot water heater, there was a tiny fireplace at one end of this huge living room, ridiculous for keeping the place warm.
We had a landing that was big enough to put a kitchen cabinet in where we kept our food. We had no fridge or larder apart from the metal cabinet we bought ourselves. The bedroom was just big enough for our bed, a small bed, wardrobe and dressing table. We had to share the toilet with the man and wife, who were Scottish, on the next floor down. It wasn't very pleasant. They were for everlasting cooking kippers and onions and all the smells came rising up to us in the flat above. There was no room for a table and chair in the kitchen so we sat awkwardly at the bath lid to eat our food in the winter. We lived in this tiny kitchen

in the winter because we could keep warm with the gas oven on, the living room was so draughty with all those windows, none of which fitted properly.

We had our coal bunker in the cellar and Reg would have to carry the coal up five flights of stairs to our top landing. There were three coal bunkers together which were about six feet high and open at the top. We didn't use our living room much in the winter because it was too cold even with the fire burning. The wind would blow through the five windows and the draughts would get everywhere.

We soon realised that our coal was going at an alarming rate with only one possible explanation, the Irish family living on the ground floor. The Scots couple never had any coal in their bunker at any time, we presumed they used electric fires or sat in their kitchen the same as we did.

We were fortunate, I suppose, that we had our own place, such as it was, and after all we would only be there temporarily until we moved into a new flat. Mum knew an American who had married an English girl while he was stationed here and had furnished a house for his bride. Now that the war was over he was selling everything and taking his bride back to America. So, with Mum's help we bought some furniture from him, a bedroom suite, a bed, a three-piece suite and some useful kitchen bits and pieces. We were very lucky because he didn't charge us too much. He probably knew that we didn't have too much to spend anyway. You had to have dockets to buy furniture just after the war. Everything was in short supply and even second-hand furniture was hard to come by, don't forget all the destruction due to the bombing.

So now I was a pregnant newly married housewife, and for the first time in my life, I had to cook and keep house for a family. Difficult, to say the least, what with food rationing and a shortage of cash. We moved in and set to work decorating and cleaning, trying to make a comfortable home.

The council sent some workmen round to put up some wallpaper, they were there for days, after all they were only doing two rooms, and I had already done the painting. When the Friday came, they still hadn't finished and they said "See you on Monday love, we should be finished by next week". That's what they think I thought. When they came back on the Monday, I opened the door to them and said "You needn't bother to come in, the wallpapering is finished". They were mad, but I had finished it.

My baby was due, then suddenly I was in King's College Hospital, two days in labour, but then I delivered a beautiful baby girl weighing eight and a half pounds. My daughter was my pride and joy, I loved her the moment she was in my arms. My mind was set on the name of Jeanie, but Mum (Reg's mum) wanted to call her Ann and so Ann she is, I loved Mum and wanted to please her.

CHAPTER 6
Bringing Up Baby

Ann

Ann was a good baby, I had lots of milk so she fed well, slept well, no problems. She learnt to walk at 9 months and was feeding herself very early. She fed herself so daintily and would never wear a bib whilst doing so. I had lots of time to care for her, she was never out of my sight but I had to find work, I had the time and it was necessary to bring some more money into the home.

There were baby minders nearby who would have her but she was my first child, and I didn't want to leave her, so I found a job locally as a house cleaner where I could take her with me. I thought it was too good to be true until I realised why the lady was taking me with a child, it was because nobody in their right mind would do the amount of work she required.

She took in men lodgers, there were ten bedrooms to keep clean and tidy every day. Aren't men untidy? A lounge, dining room, kitchen, scullery, two bathrooms and toilets. I had to do all the washing by hand in a tin bath, when the beds were changed once a week there were eleven sets of sheets, including hers, pillowcases to be washed and blued, plus towels and teacloths etc.

Hanging the washing out on the lines in the winter was really cold hard work and rinsing the washing in cold water by hand meant my hands were chapped and sore, no washing machine or dryers in those days. This was followed by the ironing.

Going home to my own housework and shopping and cooking left me absolutely drained. Although I wanted to earn the money such as it was, I couldn't carry on any longer. I never let on to Reg how much I was doing, he wouldn't have stood for it.

I found myself another job with a language teacher, she was also within walking distance of our flat and I could take Ann with me. It was cleaning again but not so hard, no lodgers, just two people lived there, but still all the washing and ironing including all the clothes they wore. I wasn't there very long when she asked me to come back in the evenings to serve her foreign guests who were learning to speak English.

I had to pass round snacks and sandwiches and drinks and talk to them to encourage them to speak our language, then I had to clear up afterwards. She would give me a small tip after each evening, but no extra wages for the evening work which she had once a week. I didn't stay long there either, it seems people who take you on with a child think that you'll put up with anything to earn a living.

I had made a friend who lived on the top floor in the house opposite mine, she had a little girl the same age as my Ann. We were in the park with the girls when we discovered that we both needed some money to make ends meet, so we came to a great decision, we could go to work and look after each other's children. I would go in the mornings and she would go in the afternoons so that we wouldn't have to pay a child minder half of what we earned.

Jobs were easy to find after the war and the first job I applied for was with a small business in a three storey house which was making plastic jewellery. I got the job and the good thing about it was it was only 5 minute's walk away from Nan's. Nan was so pleased, she wanted me to go in for my lunch every day, she always had her main meal lunchtime, and having me going in gave her someone to care for, to cook for and talk to. At this time, she was living on her own because Emmie had found herself a new husband.

This didn't come about for about a year because I was only working part time and had to get home to let my friend get to work. So, I started work in the office, I did everything that had to be done, I was the only office worker so of course everything, including wages, was up to me.

There was only one machine and that was a typewriter. The ledgers and figure work had to be done using your own brains, no adding machines etc. then, no decimal currency, there was the old fashioned £.S.D. I loved my work, I was happy. We only had seven staff and a Rep who was also the manager. This was a very new business and the plastic earrings and brooches were manufactured all by hand. I'll come back to this later for I was 17 years in this job and I can't let it go by with just a few words.

At home we were doing our best, Reg and I, to make something of our lives. We loved each other very much, then and always. Reg worked long and hard, he was now doing overtime as much as he could get. He would leave for work at seven in the morning and get home at a quarter to ten at night, that's the time we had our main meal.

There was no news about our new flat, it seemed hopeless to get rehoused. We were told that we had enough room until we had another baby and that was out of the question at that time. The other people in our house didn't ever bother to put any lino or carpet on the floor in the hall or on the stairs, but we carpeted our top two flights. When we went home it was like walking into an empty house.

We had to go up five flights of stairs, everything had to be carried, including Ann, before she could walk. Our back garden was a playground concreted over, don't forget this had been a school. I had to walk through the Irish lady's kitchen to empty our rubbish and hang out my washing, up and down the stairs again, no wonder I only weighed eight stones.

The Irish lady was married to a painter and decorator, they had two babies who always looked as if they wanted a good wash, they were very poor. She was really nice looking but never bothered to keep clean and tidy. Her place was a mess, she did nothing all day except read cheap novels.

Nearly every night when Reg was due to come home, she would come knocking on my door to have a chat and would want to taste the food I had cooked. She would ask me to give her anything left over for the children's dinner next day because they were hungry. When I made a stew, she would use the remains and just add lots of potatoes so that they could all eat it. I hated this, I found myself cooking extra, we weren't much better off than they were, but I had pity on the children.

The final straw came when Reg had his new gloves stolen which were a Christmas present from his sister and had never been worn. At this time, we were gradually losing food from the cabinet which was out on the landing. It was obvious, as we could only buy what we needed each day, because we had no fridge, so food had to be purchased the same day more or less. We made sure that they heard our conversation when we went downstairs to get coal. Reg said he was going to the Police about his gloves, and what do you know, the gloves were put back in the drawer the next time that we looked, but there were little paint splashes over them.

Reg worked hard all the week and so did I. In the football season he would go to Chelsea with his uncle to watch the football on Saturday afternoon, straight from work. Reg was always into sport. When he was at school he was in the football, cricket and boxing teams and was captain of the athletics team. Once he ran at Crystal Palace for the inter-school finals and he won a medal. The teacher gave him a huge shield to take home but he said "I'm not carrying that heavy thing home with me, it's too big". In the school sports the other boys didn't like to race against him because none had ever passed him. I think that, of all the sports, football was his favourite, he used to play sometimes three games at the weekend, I went to watch him sometimes when we first started to go out together. Apart from going to the cinema now and again we didn't have much entertainment.

At the bottom of our road we could pick up a coach and go to the seaside, so sometimes on a Saturday I would take Ann to the seaside to Southend-on-Sea. I would take sandwiches for our lunch and would buy a drink there. They never charged for Ann as long as she could sit on my lap. We loved the outing, the sand and the sea, and especially the ice cream cones, Rossi ice cream. I've never tasted ice cream like it since.

Reg's Mum

Every Sunday afternoon we caught the tram to Mum's. We always had Sunday tea with Reg's Mum and Dad, and afterwards we would put Ann to sleep in their bed and play cards. Someone always turned up to join us, all the family used Mum's house as a meeting place, she was really the head of the family, and it was a big one. We only played for pennies, just for the fun of it - Mum nearly always cheated, but we knew and laughed about it.

CHAPTER 7
We Decide to Save for a House

We had decided, our great decision, we would save hard to buy our own house. It seemed the only way we could get out of the place where we were. Reg was working all the hours he could get so I had to think about doing full time work. As it happens, we were getting very busy. My boss was a lovely man and not young anymore, he used to take his dog to work with him who was just as old as he was. He was delighted when I asked if I could work full time, not always in the office, there wasn't enough work for that but there was plenty to do.

We started to employ more girls and women as we got busier, the orders were coming in, our jewellery was very pretty and became popular.

Over the next few years our staff grew to 100, lots of them were outworkers.
I used to teach the various jobs to the new girls and was kept extremely busy with the increase in the office work. I started to take work home in the evenings, sticking stones in the earrings and brooches, all sorts of jobs including painting. I used to do the wages at home because that was the only place I could have peace and quiet to work out the outworkers' pay from their little books, and also do the wages for the rest of the staff.

My boss was generous, he knew how hard I worked and treated me accordingly. I was only twenty-three years old, and here I was responsible for so much.

I was now a member of the Stork Club at Streatham. I used to take clients there for an expensive lunch. I always used the same waiter and clients were impressed with the service they got.

Some of our clients came from Belfast twice a year, they owned a chain of gift shops, and used to spend a fair bit of money every time they came to see our new range. The presents they used to bring me, dolls and toys for Ann, every clock we owned came from Mr. & Mrs. Enlander, and she always bought me a cake which she had baked herself. Christmas time she would send the biggest turkey to me at work, and we would have a party for the staff. I made turkey sandwiches and the bones used to be picked clean.

I got on well with all of the staff and although most of them were older than me they always looked to me for advice about something or other. I understood if their children were sick and they couldn't come to work, of if they had to go to the doctor or dentist or whatever, their job was still waiting for them when they came back. They didn't get paid if they were away because they had sick children, but I made sure they got some homework to tide them over.

We were a happy bunch of people and all got on well with each other. My boss spent his days sitting mounting the jewellery on cards and pads every day and he signed the cheques. You would never think that it was his business, he never answered the phone, or saw any customers when they called, he looked like the odd job man, but I liked him very much.

CHAPTER 8
Discovering the Truth About My Birth -My Mum Dies

I had a terrible shock, my own mum came to see us, she didn't come all that often and I was always pleased to see her. The day before when I was having lunch with Nan she was upset because she had a row with Dad about something or other and she blurted out that he was not my father. I was stunned and went back to work without asking any questions, so when Mum came round I told her what Nan had said, and she burst into tears.

My real father was my uncle Bob who was my auntie Nin's husband.
I knew none of this whilst growing up, I was now twenty-three and although I started my story with my true birth I never knew until now. I wasn't really brought up by my parents and most of my life I lived with Nan and Granddad and the rest of the family, so just imagine my feelings when I discovered that I was illegitimate. Mum couldn't tell me anymore because she was crying and too upset to talk about it.

When Reg came home he found me in tears, then he told me that he had known all the time because my Nan had told his Mum and she had told him. He never mentioned it, neither did anyone else, he just comforted me and loved me and said it didn't matter, he loved me from the first meeting and would always love me and that's true after fifty years of marriage. The man my mother married never loved me, he never held me or sat me on his lap or kissed me, he never talked to me or told me stories, my granddad did all those things. He never made a home for me and my Mum.

It was much later that I found out why my mother kept having my stepfather back when he left her because of his gambling debts, and why we never lived together very long, and why she would go off with him and leave me with Nan and Granddad, it was because he blackmailed her and threatened to tell me that I wasn't his child. My Auntie Florrie told me all about everything before she died, just imagine that big family all knowing everything about me and not telling me the truth.

Now that I knew, Mum sent him packing back to his mother and wanted to move where he couldn't find her. She answered an advertisement for a live-in housekeeper, and when she went to see the man it turned out to be a boyfriend she had when she was a girl. His wife had died and he was very lonely so she moved in with him. He had a motor bike and used to take her on the back to all sorts of places, they were very happy, and I was so pleased to see her enjoying herself.

After about a year, my Mum became very ill, she was 52. I was so worried, she seemed to be wasting away. Her doctor said she had bronchitis and gave her some cough medicine. I was shocked the last time I went to see her, the doctor was there and said that there was nothing he could do. I wrapped her in a blanket and took her to the local hospital which was a small cottage hospital in Norwood. They refused to see her because she did not have a doctor's letter, so I said that we wouldn't leave until she had been examined by a doctor.

All the patients had been seen to, Mum was lying on a form with her head in my lap, we had been there for hours. Mum was distressed and wanted to go home to bed but I insisted we stay until she had been seen to. Everyone had disappeared, there wasn't a soul in sight until one nurse, who was getting just as upset as I was, called a doctor. The doctor had her sent to hospital in Croydon, where she was kept in. They gave her all sorts of drugs, lumber punctures etc. She had leukaemia and she was very ill but did recover and go into remission just before Christmas.

I asked the doctor if I could take her home for Christmas, it would be her last one, she was able to walk a little, so he agreed. She had a wonderful Christmas with us, we had lots of visitors call, they didn't stay long because they didn't want to tire her. After our Christmas lunch, we took the presents off the tree. Mum was delighted with all the lovely things she got, a new nighty, slippers, dressing gown, toilet things, chocolates, etc. "You are all so good to me" she said. "Anyone would think that I was going to die". I left the room quickly, making the excuse that I needed the toilet.

She was only well for a short time, but we all needed that time together before the end. Just before she died she managed to talk to me. "I would love some lilac love, do you think you could get me some?". There was no lilac growing in this country at this time of the year, so I got in touch with Reg's Mum, who worked in Victoria, to see if she had any ideas.

She went to the most expensive florist in London and explained what she wanted this lilac for. They said they would have to send for some from abroad, which they did. It took three days for it to arrive, and when it did, I took time off from work to take it to her. She clasped it to her breast, she was smiling when she looked at me, I held her hand while she went to sleep. My Mum never woke up again, she passed away two nights later whilst I was with her, she was still holding the lilac in her hand.

I had a job to find a nurse, or anyone, the place seemed to be deserted. This was a
hospice where they sent people to die, there should have been someone in case of emergencies. I did eventually find a nurse who was most put out because I had disturbed her tea break.
I went into the chapel to talk to the Lord, I thanked him for taking her and putting her out of her misery so quietly.

All her brothers and sisters came to the funeral, we couldn't afford a big affair. Mum was there for me, helping as usual. My uncle Alf offered to help with the expenses which I was quite moved about, but I said "No", this was the last thing that I could do for her and I wanted to do it alone.

Mum had no insurance, no money, she didn't even have a wedding ring, she had sold everything she owned when Harry was ill.

The day of the funeral was bad for me, you see I hadn't cried, I had kept it all bottled up inside.

Mum had wanted to be cremated and her ashes scattered under the trees, so when they were carrying her coffin into the chapel at the crematorium, I broke down and fell on the coffin in grief, I couldn't stand up, I had to be held. I was thinking how much she had suffered all her life, because of me. An unmarried mother married to a gambler who blackmailed her into letting him return to her life of misery. My mother was a nice person, and although I didn't know her very well, she must have loved me, she never gave me away. I mustn't write anymore about this, it's making me cry.

Since I found out that my uncle Bob was my real father, I couldn't go to his house and see my half brothers and sisters, I was so ashamed, although it wasn't my fault. I didn't tell them that I had found out, I don't even know if my half brothers and sisters knew the truth about me, I just couldn't go there anymore. Over all these years I have only seen them about half a dozen times, the only contact we have is a Christmas card every year. They live too far away, it's too late now, instead of being an only child I could have had 4 brothers and sisters. a crowd of nieces and nephews, and even great nieces and nephews as well. There isn't a week that goes by when I don't think about them, Bob, Rene, Stella and Allen. I cry as I write this, I do wish that I hadn't been so stupid to cut myself off from them.

CHAPTER 9
Billy Graham at Wembley

It's a funny thing though, my Nan always insisted that babies should be baptised in church, and you should be married in church too. I too like to listen to the services on the radio on Sunday mornings, and I became interested to find out more. I heard that Billy Graham, the well-known preacher, was coming to Wembley Stadium. He was much loved by everyone who heard him, and I wanted to see him. I asked a friend of mine if she would come with me because I would never go alone, and after some persuasion she agreed.

We had never seen so many people, all going in the same direction, and by the time we got there the only seats left were right at the top of the arena. From the moment we entered a remarkable feeling came over me, I can't really describe what it was, but I felt excited that something wonderful was going to happen.

There were thousands of people of all nationalities gathering for what was going to mean a great change in my life. The place was packed, my friend and me sitting right at the top, had a grandstand view of everything that was happening. There was a quiet anticipation all around us, then the singing began. You have never heard hymns sung like it anywhere, our voices rose up to the sky filling us with a great joy to be there. Billy Graham appeared and the silence as we listened to his words was awesome. When he called for people to come down to accept the Lord, I sat still. I felt an overwhelming desire to go down with the hundreds of others, but I remained sitting until I just had to go down. For a long time afterwards, I felt happy and wanted to be a Christian in the true sense of the word. I had made a commitment but still I did not go to church every week, I often popped into church on my own when the church was empty. I would sit and pray for a little while. I did this when my mother died, also my father and grandparents. I felt a comfort by being in the house of the Lord.

CHAPTER 10
Ann's Scarlet Fever Scare

Ann

Ann was three years old and was having bouts of tonsillitis, so the hospital advised that she had her tonsils out. When I took her in she cried non-stop. I was so worried, I didn't want to leave her.

They wouldn't allow you to stay with your babies in those days, it was visiting times only. Next day they were going to operate and I was there next day waiting for the visiting hour so that I could be with my baby.

First in the ward and what a shock I got, she had blood in her hair and on her face, the gown she wore was stained. I picked her up and told the sister that I was taking her home. If they couldn't look after her better than that she was much better off with me nursing her.

I hadn't taken any clothes for her with me and I couldn't take her on a tram or bus so I asked them to phone for a taxi and whilst we were waiting, I cleaned Ann up. All the time Ann clung to me afraid that I would leave her again. I shall never forget her face, tear lined and bloody, was it necessary to have her in that state, it distressed me more than I can say.

I made up my mind to have a big Christmas party for Ann, she had never had a party yet, after all she was only three but by Christmas, she would be four.
I bought a really nice toy each week for the 18 children I was going to invite, buying one at a time I could afford them. I made little crepe bags and filled them with sweets and I bought balloons, one for each child. All the children of Ann's age along the street were invited and then I borrowed some trestle tables and forms from the local chapel just across the road from us.

I had this very large living room, ideal for a party, which we decorated with garlands, balloons and tinsel, together with the largest tree that I could get in. Reg's cousin was coming as Father Christmas to hand out the presents, and it was wonderful the way he held each child on his knee and talked to them.

All the kids were thrilled to bits and most had never been to a party before. The look on their faces, if only I had a camera, but I never thought about buying one then. All the things we needed to live, and all that money spent giving a good time to 18 kids, but I loved it and although I was worn out at the end of the day, I went to bed happy in the knowledge that all the kids had thoroughly enjoyed the food and games and the presents from Santa Claus and the goodies to take home. One little girl didn't want to go home, twice she came back and had to be taken home again

I was so glad that I had that party for Ann because shortly after she became ill. Ann had the usual children's complaints but when she was four, she became very ill so I sent for the Doctor. He was a big German doctor who I had never seen before and he was very cross that I had sent for him, he said that she was playing up because she was an only child. My Ann never played up, she was always contented and happy, we had lots of cuddles and playtimes and outings together. I had run down to the phone box with a coat over my nightie to bring the doctor out late at night. He came much later. I expect that was why he was so cross. He didn't give her any medication, told me to give her half an aspirin to cool down her temperature.

My baby was critically ill, it's a good job that I had some nursing experience due to my voluntary work at King's

College Hospital during the war. I was distraught, the doctor wouldn't come again. He said that she would be better in a day or two. He only came that one time. I moved her bed into the living room and I slept when I could on the sofa. I hung a blanket with disinfectant over the door because if it was contagious, I didn't want Reg to catch it. I had no idea what was wrong with her, all I could do was keep bathing her and try to get some liquid into her, to comfort her, although at times she was semi-conscious. Four days later she was a little better.

Mum came round to see us, she took one look at Ann and immediately said she had Scarlet Fever, her hands and feet were skinning. Mum went out to phone the doctor and told him what she thought - he arrived 10 minutes later and confirmed her suspicions, saying "We have slipped up here mother". I could have strangled him. He sent for an ambulance to take Ann away to isolation and a fumigation truck to see to our flat.

When the men saw what I had done with everything clean and disinfected, they decided not to fumigate the flat and only took away Ann's clothes, bed linen and mattress to bake. I refused to let Ann go as she was over the crises point. As I had Scarlet Fever myself when I was a child, I was immune. I could nurse her better at home with one to one nursing and she wouldn't fret being away from me.

In those days Scarlet Fever was a killer, when I had it, I was ill for two weeks and then sent to convalesce in the country for two weeks. My Ann got better much quicker than that thank the Lord.

Ann wouldn't eat hardly a thing when she was recovering, the only thing she liked was mash and liquor and that had to be eaten in the pie and mash shop in Brixton market. Each day I would put her in her pram and walk the three miles to the pie shop, she would have mash and liquor for 10 days. I got fed up with the same food and gradually got her back to more sensible eating.

Ann was ready to start school when she was five years old, her baby minder at that time used to take children to school and collect them afterwards and keep them until their mothers came home from work. For this she wanted £2 per week and £4 when they were on holiday from school. These prices were much too high in those days, lots of working mums only got about £6 per week working full time. I got more because of all the work I was doing and I did have a responsible job.

I worked in Tulse Hill, West Norwood, which is just walking distance from a private school in Dulwich, called Oakfield. Reg's nephew went there as a boarder, it is a very good school. So, for the £2 per week that lady minder wanted, Ann could go to a private school and get a good education. They also kept children until 5 0'clock when I would walk and pick her up, no car for us in those days, buses and trams were our transport. It worked very well after the first week. She wasn't very happy at first, she just cried and cried for her mummy. I did begin to feel worried that they would say she couldn't stay on but after that she settled down nicely and became popular with the other children., She did very well with her lessons for which I was well pleased, mind you keeping up with the others with regard to uniforms, P.T. kit etc. was hard. There seemed to be a lot of extras but I managed somehow.

CHAPTER 11
Holiday Princess

Every year we went away to a holiday camp for a fortnight, we had some wonderful times. The reason we splashed out on a holiday was because we worked so hard all the year and our holiday was something special to look forward to.

Going to holiday camps meant that we could put Ann to bed so that we could go to the dance hall or watch the shows without worrying if Ann was all right. They had baby wardens checking on the youngsters every night at no extra charge and if the baby was awake and crying they would announce it over the tannoy system. Even so, Reg and I would take it in turns to nip back and see for ourselves that she was all right. She never woke up once in all those years, how could she after the hectic time she had during the day? Most of our days were used up playing with her.

I made all the costumes for the fancy dress competitions where she usually came in the first three so won a prize. We entered her for the junior holiday princess competition and only twice did she fail to come first. The last time she entered she was 14 and she won again. A lovely child was my Ann, a trim figure and a lovely smile. I treasure the photographs I have of her especially the ones where she was winning her prizes.

Reg was one for sitting on the sideline and just enjoying watching. I would enter everything, the ladies' netball team, the football team, the ladies entertainment committee. I went in for anything that was happening but most of all I loved to dance. I would dance every dance and not stop until the band stopped playing.

I remember that we were on holiday at a Camp called Little Canada on the Isle of Wight.
I got a lovely black eye playing netball against another camp, a great big lump of a lady put her elbow in my eye. I had to wear my sunglasses for a few days until the blackness went away a little.

The next day they were to choose the holiday princess around the pool, so there we all gathered, the lovely young ladies all in their best costumes and high heels ready to enter but after 10 minutes no one had stood up because they were all waiting for someone to get up first, being a little shy.
Some of the lads who we had made friends with pushed me forward to start the procession, so I paraded extravagantly around, drawing the young ladies with me. I strutted as if I were on a catwalk, just for the fun of it - black eye and all. It wasn't fair really because I was voted in as the holiday princess, me a mum of 28 against all these lovely young girls of 16 to 21.

Ann had her picture taken with me wearing the sash which is still in my photo album, she was so proud and hugged and kissed me saying she always knew that I was the best mum. That was our best holiday ever, even the weather was perfect.

CHAPTER 12
Our Own House at Last – I Pass My Driving Test

We had been in this grotty flat for 7 years and thought we had saved enough to put down a deposit on a house. Reg went to the building societies to try to raise a mortgage but was turned down by them all. In those days building societies didn't take into account overtime earned or wife's earnings so Reg's flat rate wage wasn't enough.

Our disappointment on hearing this was to say the least shattering. At this time a lot of foreign people had started to move into our street, these were big houses and once used to house well-to-do people, now there seemed to be dozens of them living in each house, as one filled up so the locals would move out and more foreigners would move in. We weren't used to living with them, they didn't behave like us and quite honestly, I was scared many times. I had unrepeatable things called out to me as I had to walk past on my way home, so not being able to move out ourselves was very upsetting.

Now was the busy time looking for a house. We had made up our minds that we wanted to live near Crystal Palace because the air was cleaner than in any other part of London and its suburbs (Reg had asthma when he came out of the Air Force, and after all the tests the doctors advised him to live at a higher altitude where the air was fresher.)

Reg was telling one of his mates at work our difficulty in getting a mortgage, when he said " Why don't you go to Croydon Council, they have money to lend ex-servicemen?" So, our hopes were built up again. Reg applied for a loan, and what do you know, they had so much money to lend, people were just not asking for it, so we were promised a loan at a much lower rate than the regular building societies. In those days, 1955, you could buy a very nice terraced house in good repair, three bedrooms, lounge, kitchen dining room, bathroom, garden back and front for £1,800 but where we wanted to live there was nothing available that we liked.

We opted to buy a new house after seeing the plans at the estate agents - the houses were just starting to be built, the price £2,700. Our contract was signed with the Council stating a date when we had to move in, otherwise we would have to have a new contract probably at a rate not so good as the one we would get then.

Week after week we would get on the bus to go and have a look at how the builders were getting on. It's exciting watching your own house taking shape, but was it going to be ready on time? They were building 11 houses and were doing a little on each, ours was the one right in the middle, a semi-detached house, was it going to be ready on time? Only a few weeks to go and we were nearly out of time. I saw the boss of the site and told him about how we would lose out if the house wasn't completed on time and, after a little persuasion, he agreed to finish our house first. We moved in on a cold and wet November day with the paint still wet, they had only finished that same morning. We sat in the middle of our lounge eating fish and chips out of paper with the removal men. When they had gone, we found that we had exactly 10 shillings to last us until the end of the week when we both got our weekly wages, but it was worth it.

We were buying our own home, we still had to work hard to pay for it and everyone was saying that we were mad putting a debt like that over our heads. None of our relations owned their own houses. We were on our way, Reg and I, a long way to go but we were getting there.

At work the jewellery business was growing, we bought the house next door to expand, we also bought a metal plating works about 2 miles away to do our plating, because at this time we were making lots of metal jewellery combined with plastic which had become very popular.

Mr. Thompson, my boss, put his younger son in charge of the plating works, he made a good job of it even managing to do plating for other customers as well. All those pixies and lucky charms that you could buy at the seaside came from our firm, lots of holiday shops had a large selection of our jewellery.

I thought that it would be great if we could get into Woolworth's, but as much as I tried I couldn't get an interview with the buyer. I thought up a plan, I found out what his name was and made up my mind. What did I have to lose? so here is what I did. I put on my best clothes, did my hair extra smart and went along to their offices in Norbury. I got into the secretary's office, introduced myself, and said that I had an appointment. The secretary looked in her book, of course she couldn't find it, it wasn't there. "Just a moment" she said, and went into the buyer's office. I edged a bit nearer so that I could hear what she was saying. "There is a young lady out here who says she has an appointment, a Mrs. Lawrence. "I haven't got any appointment with anyone" he said. "What's she look like?" "She's nice looking" said the secretary. "I might as well see her now that she is here". I moved away from the door as the secretary came out to show me in. I explained to him what I had done, I said that I had been trying to get an appointment for ages, and I was sure that when he saw what I had to show him, he would be very interested. He grinned, "Let's see what you have got then". He liked the jewellery very much and gave me a very decent order, so I was overjoyed to go back to work and tell Mr.Thompson my boss.

We got into Woolworths, great, we were made! There weren't enough hours in the day to produce all the stuff that Woolworths wanted, they pressed us for more and more and quicker deliveries. Some of our customers were being neglected, good customers who paid more than Woolworth's did, but we had to supply our biggest customer now that we had taken on so much in extra overheads.

Our manager and I would often go to work on Saturday and sometimes Sunday, if Reg was working, so that we could do the costing on the new range of jewellery. We had a new range twice a year which we designed ourselves.

My boss asked me to take some driving lessons, which he would pay for, because it would be useful for urgent deliveries in town. We only had one car in the firm and that was the rep's. Mr. Thompson used to be picked up each morning and taken home at night so he didn't want to drive, besides he was a little too old to start learning even if he had wanted to. I booked up for 10 lessons which cost £10 to be paid in advance. I went for my first lesson, the lady instructor said I should fill in the form for a test straight away because there was a long waiting list. I had my first 3 lessons the first week and then I got a letter saying that my test was in one week's time, ridiculous.

I had yet to learn all the highway code apart from how to drive the car. So, we crammed in five more lessons, one each day, and I decided to take the test so that I would know what to expect when I took the real test. I was only going to use the test as another lesson, no way did I think I was ready after 8 lessons (8 lessons in two weeks).

Quite confident, I followed instructions as to where to go, no nerves, why should I have, this was just another driving lesson? I pulled out into heavy traffic almost immediately and continued until it was time to do an emergency stop. The examiner took us around into a side street and said that when he tapped the dashboard I was to stop, but before he could do so two small children holding hands walked right in front of the car. I stopped, the examiner hit his head on the dashboard (there were no safety belts in those days) and all my shopping was thrown onto the floor. I got out of the car and took the two children across the road to safety telling them what they had done wrong.

The examiner was sitting nursing his sore head, "what shall I do now?" I asked.
So, we drove back to the driving centre where he asked me a few questions, and guess what, he gave me a pass!

I had passed the driving test with just 8 lessons, nobody would believe me until I showed them the pink slip, my boss astounded me by giving me the rep's car which he said he was going to give me for a Christmas present. This was in October, which by the way is my birthday month, so he gave it to me for my birthday instead. I wasn't prepared to drive the car alone so I used to take it out and practice a bit more road work around the quiet streets until I felt more competent, and safe.

My first car was a second-hand one, but mine, wasn't that wonderful? Driving to work, not having to walk up a very long steep hill and wait in all weathers for buses, no heavy shopping to carry about. I was 28 and I have had a car ever since. By the way my boss gave me £100 as a Christmas present, an awful lot of money then.

CHAPTER 13
Reg's Dad Dies

We had a lot to do in our new house especially the garden. We had a very large garden and first of all we had to clear the woods that our house had been built on before we could plan a garden. Apart from all the undergrowth, blackberry bushes etc. we had three huge oak trees and some smaller trees to clear, and with the help of our next door neighbour who was a foreman on a building site, and as strong as an ox, we cleared it. Mind you it took some time because we were still working flat out to pay all our new expenses.

Instead of 18/6 per week rent we had to find £4.10 to cover rates, mortgage and on top of that school fees. There seemed to be no end to the expenses when you are a house owner, or should I say a housebuyer.

Reg wasn't very happy at work, such long hours, so he decided to apply for a summer relief job at The Daily Express newspaper. If you could get into a newspaper that was it, good pay, regular hours, one of the top jobs in the printing industry. Even if he was successful, it would have meant he only had work for that summer period and it was a bit of a gamble because he had to give up his other full-time job, although there was a chance he could be kept on permanently. He was taken on as a temp for the holiday period hoping that he would be kept on afterwards. It was

April 1958 and, when he left at the end of the holidays in October, his Dad died of cancer on the same day. What a day, you lose your job and your Dad all the same day, how hard can life be?

When Reg's Dad died his Mum was left to run a Public house. They had only taken over the place a few months before. It was Dad's ambition to run a Pub for the last years of his life, so when Dad collapsed one night after never even being ill (I can never remember Dad being ill in his life) when he was diagnosed as having cancer it was a terrible shock.

Whilst Dad was away in hospital Reg and I would go and help Mum in the pub, it wasn't at all the sort of life we would like to have, but Mum asked us to move in with her so that she could keep the pub on. I loved my job and my home and to serve in a pub and clean up every day in a smelly pub wasn't my idea of the good life to which Reg entirely agreed. He hated it as much as me, what sort of a life would a child have with not even a garden to play in?

When Mum sold out (they had been tenants) it meant that she had lost most of her life savings, she came and lived with us and it was a joy to have her.

When the summer relief job had finished, Reg was out of work for a few weeks and each day we would watch for the post hoping for a letter from the newspaper asking him to come back. Then when we had resigned ourselves to the fact that it wasn't going to come, we booked to go on holiday for one week to a holiday camp. The following February Reg was called back for a permanent position as a compositor on days. This now meant he could not come on holiday with us in the summer so I took one of Ann's school friends with us instead, while Reg worked and had to look after himself at home. When we arrived at the camp, we saw there was a lovely dance floor and band every night so we went along and sat in the front row after dinner. I love dancing and, in those days, you couldn't get up and dance on your own but needed a partner. The music started and I was tapping my feet wishing I could dance with someone as Reg wasn't there. After the interval a lot more people came in and the dance hall was full. I was still tapping my feet when a distinguished looking young man, wearing a white suit, came over to me and held out his hand and said 'dance?'. At this point the leader of the band said 'the next dance is going to be a tango' and nobody got up to dance, not one person, but this handsome young man dressed in his smart white suit led me to the centre of the dance floor and we danced like I have never danced before! It was absolutely fantastic, we had the whole dance floor to ourselves and I felt as though I was dancing on air. The music stopped and everybody stood up and clapped and the young man just disappeared.

I do believe I had danced with my Angel because we couldn't find him and never saw him again.

As things worked out, we didn't do too bad and Reg was always on days which meant he had to get up at 5 a.m. but was home early, he also had his two days off during the week. Monday and Tuesday one week, Tuesday and Wednesday the next and so on which meant he had one full week-end every six weeks.

Ann dearly wanted a puppy so, because someone was nearly always at home, we bought her a miniature Poodle which we named Tandy. She was chocolate brown in colour and was the happiest little thing and the prettiest that you ever did see. She quickly took over our hearts, Ann taught her tricks, she used to dress her up and Tandy would dance around with her paws in the air. We let her have pups just once on the advice of the vet, when she became a bit broody. We had her mated with a pedigree dog, the fee would be more than covered when we sold the pups, so that was all right.

I was still going into Nan's most days and she looked after Tandy whilst I was at work, until the pups were born at Nan's during the day, three brown and one apricot colour. Tandy went on to live to be a great age. When she died, I swore that I would never have another dog, it was so heartbreaking to lose her.

CHAPTER 14
I Have a Lovely Son

What do they say about new house new baby? Yes, I became pregnant, it was 1958. I love children and would have loved to have a large family so, although I was bit fearful of the consequences, I looked forward with eager anticipation to another child.

I carried on working full time at the jewellery firm, when one day, whilst I was at work I collapsed in acute pain in my right side and was rushed to King's College Hospital with suspected appendicitis. I was seven months pregnant and I didn't know at the time that because of the position of the head of the baby there was a 50/50 chance that I might lose it. They were going to operate early the next morning. During the night an old lady in the same ward as me came and sat with me and held my hand and comforted me. She told me that she was an orphan because her father was a drunkard and had set light to their home burning to death 5 brothers and sisters with her Mum and Dad during the night. She was 3 years old at the time and was the only survivor. That lady was hideous, a mass of scars and wrinkled skin, it hurt to look at her but she had great courage and her voice was sweet and soothing.

She gave me a text to put under my pillow and said a prayer with me. I felt at peace and slept like a baby. In the morning I wouldn't let them prepare me for the operation because the pain had gone, so they sent for the specialist who came with all the students (this was King's College Hospital, which is also a teaching hospital) to examine me and decided to keep me in for a few days to keep an eye on me. I still have my appendix today. I went home and prepared for the birth, I just knew that I was going to have a boy. I knitted in blue and white, painted the nursery in blue and white, got everything ready for a little boy. I put on so much weight, I went from 9 stones to 13 stones.

I got so fat that I had a job turning the wheel of the car because my tummy kept touching it and when I walked, I waddled. I was still working full time although I did get very tired, but happy just the same.

The time came, back into King's and another long labour. I was having bets with the doctors and nurses that I would have a boy, so when they took me into the delivery room in the early hours of the morning, I wanted to see my son arrive. They turned me on my side with one foot in the air, then they adjusted one of the big lights so that I could see into the mirror, so I watched and there he came at 3 a.m. a beautiful fat baby boy, he slithered and plopped out all 9 and a quarter pounds of him. The doctor, only a young intern, was so excited, it was the biggest baby he had ever delivered, he went straight out to the phone in the hall to telephone Reg and tell him that he was the father of a beautiful son. In those days they wouldn't let the fathers stay, they were sent home, in Reg's case to his Mum with Ann.

I was so excited and hungry that the nurses made me a chicken sandwich and a hot drink, they sat on my bed talking through the night whilst I cuddled my wonderful new-born baby, strictly against the rules.

When Reg came with Ann next day they came with masses of Daffodils, there must have been 20 dozen, they had picked everyone from our garden, there were enough to go around all the ward.

I was the oldest Mum in the ward and the only one with a child already, so the other young mums would ask my advice about burping, nappy changing etc. We had our babies in a cot at the bottom of the bed and if they cried in the night the nurses would take them out so as not to disturb the rest of the ward.

My baby was never taken out, not once all the time I was in there. I was feeding two other premature babies with my milk. I had to wear cups to catch the surplus milk and put it into a jar beside my bed, when the cups were full, so you can see my son was very well fed and contented.

They had special times when we were supposed to feed the babies, we were not allowed to pick them up whenever we wanted, so some of the mums got fretful when their babies cried. I ignored this rule, not that my baby cried very often but when he did, I would get up and take him into bed with me.

One day I was having a cuddle when the Matron walked in with a crowd of visitors. She stopped at the end of my bed, my heart jumped in my mouth, everyone went in awe of Matron especially the nurses. She turned to the visitors with a big smile and said "We like to see the mothers looking so happy with their babies". After that the other mothers would nurse their babies whenever they felt like it, there were no recriminations.

It's strange to think that, when I was a young mother, they used to keep you in hospital for two weeks and today you are in and out in a day or two, that's progress I suppose. We named our son Anthony Edward, and I must say at this point that the two greatest blessings in my life are my two children who have brought me nothing but pleasure.

CHAPTER 15
My Nan and Granddad Die

Picking out the important things in your life, it's strange how certain things seem to linger in your mind, like the smell of certain food reminds you of things past, like rabbit stew reminds me of when I came home from convalescence when I was just a little girl, and apple pie when we all sat round the table at Nan's on Sunday tea time, skate sizzling in the pan just how Nan cooked it in butter.

Sometimes Nan would keep me home from school to keep her company when everyone was at work, or school, then she would always do herself a special breakfast, kippers or haddock with an egg on it or egg and bacon which she would share with me. I always felt that I was special with Nan and I loved her so.

Steak and kidney pudding reminds me of Granddad because that was his favourite dinner. Poor granddad, he had not been retired long when his dog 'Trouble' died. He thought the world of that dog, they were always together, if Granddad sat down, Trouble had to lay at his feet. Granddad fed her, brushed her, talked to her, he just seemed lost without her. Granddad seemed to give up, he just went to sleep one night and never woke up again.

I was pregnant with Ann at the time so I wasn't allowed to go to the funeral. You know I can never remember Granddad being ill, he was always a quiet man and just liked his half pint of Guinness with Nan every day. They were such a lovely couple, every day when he came home from work he would hold her face between his hands saying "Hello old girl" and give her a kiss. When I was little, I used to say to him, "Me too Granddad" and he used to lift me up and rub his moustache against my face before giving me a kiss.

Nan was lonely after Granddad died, no dog and no husband, all the family had left to get married, she was so used to having lots of people to care for that she decided to take in a lodger. She took in a young fellow, an Irishman, and seemed happier with some company. She did everything for him, all his washing and ironing, cooked him delicious meals, so I was extremely shocked to hear that he had tortured and raped her. It was in the papers, a terrible case, she was 64 and in those days things like that didn't happen. He was duly sent to prison, but Nan never got over it. Shortly after she was found dead with a heart attack, was it because of this or did she miss Granddad so much? How soon does one's life change. Nan's life was always busy and full of people and children, who gave her all her happiness. She never went to church, but made sure that all the children went to Sunday school. I hope that she went to heaven, she ought to.

When I had my baby, 'Tony', I was still working at the
jewellery firm so I was allowed to work at home until I felt
able to continue full time again. I had to arrange for Tony
to be looked after until he was old enough to go to school. I
found a very nice lady called Gwen who had a son of her
own, she only lived a short walk away so it was very
convenient, although I hated to leave him with someone
else.

Weekends were very busy for me, we always had a
houseful of children, both Ann and Tony preferred their
friends to come and play at our house rather than go and
play with them in theirs, perhaps it's because we had such a
large garden.

We had a full- size slide and swing, we made a putting
green with one hole in the middle of the lawn. The big
lawn was the football and cricket pitch. We had a large
patio on which we erected a fair size paddling pool with
seats on each corner for the summer, and as long as the
children were good there was no trouble to speak of. Once
when Tony was about four there was a new little boy who
came to play. Straight away he started pushing and shoving
and in general upsetting the others. He always wanted to
play with everything that other children were playing with,
always wanted to be first in everything. I sent him home
and told him he couldn't come back until he could behave
himself. He did come back the following weekend and was

never any trouble again, in fact he turned out to be a very nice lad.

My house wasn't far from the local school, the children used to pass my house on their way home, I had this large front garden and very often I would be working in it when the children came out of school. They used to pass the time chatting to me, sometimes I would pick a few flowers for them to take home to their mums. One time that comes to mind was when a little girl, who I had never seen before, fell over and grazed her knee, I knew the little girl who was with her and she asked me if I would put a bandage on her, so I took her into the kitchen, bathed and put a plaster on her knee, then I asked her where she lived "I have just moved in over the road" she said. I wondered why she didn't go home instead of coming to me but then the children often came to me with their troubles.

One time they brought me a tiny little bird that had fallen out of its nest. I made a nest for it in my greenhouse and used to dig up worms, cut them up and feed them to what turned out to be a Robin redbreast. The children used to love him and came to see how the little creature was getting on.
I taught that robin how to fly when it was old enough, by putting it on the window ledge outside my kitchen, then I gently pushed it off. The first few times it fluttered to the ground. but it was surprising how quickly it got the idea and was soon flying all around the garden. That Robin

stayed with us for years, it used to peck on the kitchen window in the mornings for me to feed it.

Another time we had a Duck and a Drake who decided to make a nest the other side of our back fence, which was a wood, and we had a hole going underneath which they used to come into the garden to see what they could scrounge. We had a lovely surprise one Spring Sunday morning for there, coming down the path, was the duck and trooping behind her five little ducklings. There was a lake down the bottom of our road, and she was headed in that direction. What a sight to see, the little troop walking in the middle of the road with a group of assorted children and mums following them down to the lake. It was about a mile away, she made it with a great cheer from the following crowd. Why is it that we didn't take a photograph of the occasion?

There are so many happenings in life that you can look back on and wonder at the beauty of life.

My children always had birthday parties, whereas Ann had the traditional kind with sandwiches, ice cream, jelly and cakes, and games of course, Tony wanted just a few children to share with him a traditional lunch, like steak and kidney pie, or roast beef followed by trifle or steamed pudding and custard, he always chose what he wanted. Then we would go out, swimming or to Shirley Hills where we would play football or play follow my leader, I would be the leader and the children would have to do whatever I did, sometimes we played football when I was always put in goal. We had great times and lots of laughter, afterwards we would go home to tea. Those times we had when the children were growing up can never be repeated, you have to make the most of them because once they leave the nest it's only the memories you have left. I can honestly say that my children were happy, they had lots of cuddles and hugs and I did my best to give them the very best according to our means. People say that children should not be punished today, by punished I mean smacking, well the only punishment I gave my Ann was a little shaking now and again and my Tony was never punished. O yes, he was naughty like all children are sometimes so I used to shout at him and tell him he was a naughty boy and he would come running to me and cling to my leg and say that he wouldn't do it anymore, and he never did, he did something else instead.

What do children know about what is naughty and what isn't? It's just something they have to learn as they grow up. Tony always liked lots of hugs and kisses, even when he was 21, I remember he sat on my lap to have a hug and nearly squashed me, all 6 foot of him.

Tony was five years old, it was time to go to school, and of course he went to Oakfield, the same as Ann. She had done very well whilst she was there and was now finishing her education locally. The age difference between our two children is ten years, so it was fortunate that we didn't have two lots of school fees to pay for at the same time because in between time the prices of school fees had risen as they are inclined to do with all things.

There was one incident that I remember when Tony started school that amuses me. He became very fond of the headmaster's little girl who was in the same class. He gave her a ring that he had got out of a bonbon, so they were engaged. Her mother was having a sort out of baby clothes to give away, her daughter said, "Please don't give them away Mummy, Tony and I will be glad of them when we have our babies" They were both five years old.

CHAPTER 16
Waitressing on Celebrities

I wasn't very happy at work, my boss's son had just come out of the Navy where he had been until he retired. He joined our company which he would one day own, his brother Norman was already running the plating works and was doing very well, that would belong to him completely when his father died. The jewellery business would belong to John who was the eldest. I liked John and promised to teach him everything I knew of the business, he was a very willing pupil and we got on well.

At this time, we had employed a very nice man, who was once a fully qualified accountant, to work in the office. He was retired and worked for us part time which left me free with other business concerning manufacturing the jewellery. John started playing the Governor and began making changes which were not working out at all, different ideas as to what to do and what not to do. After two years we had to start cutting our costs because we were just not getting enough for our goods. It's a long story, but the end results were that we were gradually sacking our staff.
Some of our ladies had been with us almost from the very beginning and were in supervisory positions, whereas I used to train new staff, the supervisors did a good job running the different sections.

The final straw came when John said that the supervisors would have to go because they were earning the most money, I should think so, they had been with us as long as 14 or 15 years and earned every penny they got. I was broken hearted and decided I couldn't take any more. There were only 7 staff when I first went to work there, then the company built up to over a hundred staff.
We had bought the building next door and a plating works. My boss had bought several houses, also a villa in Malta, now we were on a decline, I couldn't see it go down anymore. I gave him an ultimatum, either they stay, or I leave.

I left, after 17 years it was time to move on. My boss old Mr. Thompson phoned me often to go back because the firm was going downhill fast, but I couldn't face seeing a firm that I had worked so hard for going down the drain.

A few weeks at home then it was time I sorted myself out and found another job. Mum said "why don't you come with me into casual waitressing, I will teach you all you need to know?". I thought about it, it sounded a good idea, for I would only have to work when I wanted to which meant that I would be home for Tony more often.

Mum was working for 5 different caterers, so she had plenty of casual work offered to her, they were only too pleased to get another name on their books, so I started. The very first job she took me on was a cocktail party. So far, so good. It didn't take much learning to hand snacks around and drinks from a tray, but was I tired after four hours of walking about and clearing up afterwards.

As time went on Mum took me on more and more jobs, all the time teaching me. She knew all there was to know about catering and I could at last go out on jobs without her. Saturdays was usually weddings, the Caterers sometimes had 25 weddings on one day. In those days if people married just before April 5th, they got a year's income tax refund. Often, I would be in charge of one of the smaller weddings. I remember one of the first weddings Mum and I did was at Clapham Baths. The guests had the cheapest wedding breakfast we had ever done, by the time we had put up the tables and chairs there was no room for us to get into the room to serve the meal properly, not that they had much, no starter, just chicken and ham salad with potatoes and a roll and butter, no sweet. We had to prepare this meal on the landing using a trestle table as a work surface and a tin bath for washing up. They had no wedding cake, no wine, just a barrel of beer. We were fed up, there's one thing that a waitress takes pride in and that's doing the job well. How could we do a job well under these terrible circumstances? We had never worked without a kitchen before. When the guests arrived and sat down we had to pass the plates of meat down the tables, the men passed the beer and caused great amusement on all sides, I must say I have never heard a happier bunch of people before, they really were having a good time much to Mum and my amazement. They didn't want any speeches, there were no cards to read out and no telegrams. Mum and I looked at each other, it didn't look as if we were going to get any tip here. We were to work for seven hours for £3.50 and we relied on our tips to make our money up. Don't forget we had to pay our fares to get to the job out of that, but of course I had a car but it still cost money to run it. At the end of the wedding, we had everything stowed away waiting for the driver to come and collect the tables and equipment. We couldn't leave until everything was taken away. The father of the bride came looking for us, he said "that was smashing girls, it was just what we wanted, you did a bloody good job, here take this". He handed us £5 each. That tip was the biggest tip we had ever received, more than a day's wages. You can never tell with people, although we have always found that the poorer the people are the more generous they tip. Some of the caterers we worked for only did top of the range jobs, such as millionaires' do's, the Guildhall and Palaces, plus lots of very wealthy functions which I will tell you about later.

Once a year we went to a hospital for incurables at Crown Point at Upper Norwood, to do a strawberry tea. We did this job voluntarily. It was heartbreaking seeing these poor people who had to have everything done for them, all were in wheelchairs and each one had a helper to feed them, some couldn't even chew properly so it took a lot of patience and time. Those who could talk a little were so thankful for all we did. I can never remember it ever raining when we were there, so that their relatives and friends who had been invited could have their tea and strawberries in the gardens and listen to the band playing,

they may have had a happy time but for me I couldn't wait
to get home and be so grateful that it wasn't one of my
loved ones living there.

We did one other job once a year without pay, and that was
at Clapham Baths for the W.V.S. The hall was quite a large
one (not like the smallest room in the place where we did
the wedding) and every Christmas we would do a
Christmas dinner and party for the old folk. We had about
20 people each to serve because not every waitress wanted
to work for nothing especially at Christmas time, so those
that did turn up had a lot to do, of course the W.V.S. ladies
helped us as well. We had to lay all the tables up before we
could serve a turkey dinner with Christmas pudding and
mince pies and custard with a cup of tea to follow.

One time one of the old ladies who Mum was serving said
to her "Could I have another mince pie please, dear, I am 65
and live on my own and don't often get a treat like this".
Mum didn't say anything, she was 75 at the time and was
running about like a two year old. Mum was still waiting
on people into her eighties, I would rather have Mum for a
partner when working than anyone else, she always pulled
her weight and never went missing to avoid the jobs that
had to be done.

You know those W.V.S. ladies are worth their weight in
gold, the amount of effort they put into everything they did
to help the aged. At this Christmas party they put on a
show, then somebody played the piano and everyone joined

in singing the old songs, some of the old folk dressed up as coster mongers with the big feathered hats. When it was time for them to go home each was given a bag of goodies, tea, sugar, biscuits, all sorts of things to fill a carrier bag. You know some were so artful, they would go out, hide their bag somewhere, then go back in by another door to get another one.

I really felt able to do anything now. Mum had taught me how to lay a table for a banquet, or for a small dinner party. I could now fold serviettes 5 different ways. I could run a bar, serve wines, do silver service and butler service. Cocktail parties were now easy but there was a lot more to come as you will discover as you read on.

CHAPTER 17
Ann's Wedding

After some time I wondered why I had to work so hard,
surely there was something I could do besides waitress
work, I really was an office worker, but where could you
get office work that would fit into being at home more often
with Tony, not Ann for she was now working and doing
very nicely being a secretary for a solicitor who was also
an M.P. I was very proud of her.

She told me a story once when she had to go to the Houses
of Parliament and the police held up the traffic to let her get
into the car park. It's always very busy in Parliament
Square in the heart of London, she said she felt like royalty
having the traffic stopped to let a junior secretary in

Ann had been going out with a boy called Duncan for some
years, his mother and father had moved to Yorkshire and as
he didn't want to go there, he had moved into furnished
lodgings sharing with a friend. Ann asked if he could come
for Sunday lunch, so of course I said yes. I have never seen
anybody eat so much, he was over six feet tall and had a
healthy appetite to go with it. He was training to be a civil
engineer, I think Ann was 18 when she met him.

After a while Duncan came round for a meal twice a week,
then it became three times a week. I said to him "I think

you must be eating for two days", he agreed and said I
shouldn't be such a good cook.

Ann's 21st birthday was coming up so Reg and I decided
that we would give her a good party. We booked The
Amigo Hall, near the Elephant and Castle, for the party and
told her she could invite all her friends, then we booked a
disc jockey. My sister-in-law and her husband, Arthur, and
Mum were going to do the catering for us. We had a
birthday cake made and everything was arranged for a
wonderful party. I was only half awake in bed on a Sunday
morning when Ann came in and sat on the bed and said that
Duncan had been offered a job in Colchester to build a new
motorway. He was now fully qualified, he wanted to get
married so that Ann could go with him to Colchester as his
bride.

This was three weeks before her 21st birthday, three weeks
to arrange a wedding when it had taken us months to
arrange her birthday party. Well, the hall was already
booked, and the music, but it was going to be on a Sunday.

The first trip was to see the vicar. Our vicar, Father Bailey,
had just retired, he was a lovely man and had taken Ann for
her lessons leading up to her confirmation. We had a new
vicar who we didn't know so we made an appointment to go
and see him to have the bans read. He refused to marry
them on a Sunday saying that it was illegal to perform
marriage services on that day. I told him that I was a

waitress and did weddings often on Sunday. He said that only applied to Italians and Jews and other nationalities.

He didn't know us, so I told him that the Archbishop of Canterbury was a friend of mine. It was true because I used to wait on the Archbishop at Lambeth Palace often and he certainly was my friend, we often had little chats for I used to be the one who waited on him. I said to this vicar "Would you like me to ask Dr. Ramsay to give you permission to marry my daughter, if you like I will phone him straight away and ask him to talk to you?" The vicar blushed scarlet and said that wouldn't be necessary, he would marry them. What a hectic three weeks to prepare everything.

We hired a bride gown and all the trimmings from the wedding hire shop. It was really beautiful and much better than we could afford if we had bought a new one. Then one of Reg's cousins lent us two velvet bridesmaids' dresses with little hats to match. Then we got busy sending out wedding invitations to the relatives. We ordered a wedding cake and the cars. We had menus printed, all with a fancy tassel. We had many family discussions as to what meal we would have and this was what we chose:

Prawn Cocktail

~~~~

Cold Roast Beef and York Ham
With Minted Potatoes
Assorted Salad

~~~

Melon Surprise
with
Fresh Cream

~~~

English Red Vein Cheese and Biscuits
Fresh Fruit
Coffee and Sweetmeats

~~~

Brandy and Liqueurs

We decided to have round tables with pink tablecloths and
pink carnations in a nice setting in the middle of each table.
Each table had an ice bucket to keep the wines cool. We
invited 80 guests for the actual wedding and the friends
who we had invited for Ann's birthday party came for the
evening buffet dance as was previously arranged.

On the Friday before the wedding, Reg's uncle Jim, who
was a taxi driver, took me at 5 0'clock in the morning to
Covent Garden Flower Market to buy the flowers to
decorate the church and the hall where the party was to be
held. He used to deliver flowers to various shops early in
the morning, so he knew quite a lot of the market traders. I
bought large Chrysanthemums for the church, small pink
carnations for the table decorations and eighty carnations to
make buttonholes for the wedding guests. The lady who we
bought the carnations from told me how to make my own
buttonholes with Maidenhead fern and not to cut the stems
off until the day of their wedding but leave them standing in

a bucket of cool water, which I did and they didn't wilt all day. Other market people gave me huge bunches of white and mauve lilac. We had so many flowers that there was hardly room for me to get in the taxi on the way home. I still remember the lovely smell of the carnations and to this day the carnation is my favourite flower.

On the Saturday before the wedding a friend of mine, who lived right opposite my house, came with me to church to help me arrange the flowers. We were there for three hours and I must say that I have never seen our church look so beautiful. Whilst we were in the church the vicar came and said "You aren't going to take the flowers away after the wedding are you?", just as if I would!

The vicar at that time was the only person to put a damper on the celebrations, if only Father Bailey was still there, it would have been a truly wonderful day.

We spent hours decorating the church, we put the lilac, pink and blue mixed into the tall pedestals going all the way from the entrance, down the aisle to the altar. We filled the steps leading up to the altar with the large chrysanthemums and carnations. This was a high church, and a very big one.

When I arrived at the church, I nearly cried, someone had moved all the pedestals holding the lilacs right to the sides of the church where you wouldn't even notice them. I just know it was that vicar.

He seemed determined to spoil our day, he didn't even shake hands with anyone after the service.
As it was, both Ann and Duncan answered him with clear and resounding voices so that everyone could hear their responses and everything turned out all right after all.

It was such a lovely wedding, everything was perfect, everyone mixed together as if they had known each other for ever. Dol and Arthur, Laurie and Irene, (Dol's son and daughter-in-law), and Mum and some of my friends, who were waitresses, did a wonderful job. We were supposed to be out of the hall by eleven O'clock but it was almost 1 O'clock before the last guest left, some visitors who came a long way even missed their last train home and had to put up in a hotel for the night. What a wedding! Being in the catering business, I knew what a success it was and I can honestly say that my Ann's wedding was the finest that I had ever seen, thanks to all the great work done by everyone. Even the Caretaker of the hall said that it was the best wedding he had ever seen, mind you we did make sure that he had a good meal and a nice drink because we had been there often doing weddings etc. and he knew us well.

Ann with her Dad (Reg)
Ann's Wedding

That night, or should I say early morning, I fell into bed and then it hit me, my Ann had gone, I felt empty inside, then I cried and fell asleep in Reg's arms.

A few days later the post arrived and with it letters from Duncan's relatives thanking us for the wonderful time they had had, I still have the letters together with the wedding photographs which I treasure.

CHAPTER 18
My Lovely Dog Max

Max

When Tony was about 10 years old, he kept pestering us to buy him a dog. He always kept on about Ann having had a dog, it wasn't fair, why couldn't he have one? Our next door neighbour had two little girls who both wanted a dog too, so she said she would look after the dog during the day when we were out.

She was French and every year went home for a month to visit her mum and dad in France so she couldn't have a dog because of that, although she was home all day and I was working full time then. So, before we went away on holiday, we ordered a West Highland Terrier, but didn't tell Tony.

When we got home from our holiday there was a letter on the mat telling us that the puppy was ready for collection. We told Tony that we were going up the road to get some shopping. When we came back Reg had the puppy inside his coat to keep it warm, you see they had just given him a bath and he looked just like a drowned rat. You should have seen the look on Tony's face when he saw him, once it had dried out it was a little white fluffy ball. We all loved our dog who we called Max. He was so clever and learned everything very quickly.

The first night we had him we made a bed for him under the table in the kitchen but, did he cry in the night. I kept going down to him and putting him back in his bed, I must have gone down half a dozen times. Eventually I stroked him until he was asleep. The next morning, there were little puddles all over the kitchen floor, I should have remembered that we had the same trouble when Ann had her poodle.

I put newspaper all over the floor the next night, then the following night I didn't put so much down. Each night I put less and less down until there was only a little bit by the back door, Max never wet the floor again, he just cried to be let out.

We made a hole underneath our fence so that he could go next door during the day, when it was time for me to leave for work he would go round and bark to be let in, then he would bound upstairs and jump on the girls licking them all over to wake them up. He stayed next door until Reg came home early in the afternoon because he started work early in the morning. So, Max had the love of two families. He also had lots of walks, there was always someone who wanted to take him for a walk round our lake.

Our road had a lake at the end of it, with a nice walk around and back again through a country lane by some allotments. We were also walking distance from Crystal Palace park, there was always something going on there to see, especially since they had built a sports centre.

When we went on holiday we took Max to stay with my daughter who, at this time, was living in Whitby. It took us all day to drive there, and he had a wonderful time. We couldn't bear to put him into kennels. When we came home again, there was another day's journey to pick him up.

Max lived to a great age, he always behaved like a puppy and could outrun even the fastest runner. He caught a germ, which at the time was killing puppies and older dogs. It was just after Christmas when we took him to the vet who prescribed some medicine and gave him a shot which didn't seem to do any good. Then the vet said he would keep him in but, it was no good, he was suffering so much that he had to be put down.

It was all over, our lovely Maxi had gone. He was 13, we missed him so much, he was more than a member of the family, he was the heart and soul of it. I'll never have another dog. I just couldn't stand the grief. One of these days I shall write a book about Maxi, I could fill lots of children's books with the capers that Maxi got up to.

CHAPTER 19
Journey in a Blizzard to See My First Grandson

I wanted a job where I could be home for my family, so after scanning the papers, I applied for a job as a cleaning supervisor. I had no training for such a job but they assured me that I would be supervised myself until I got the hang of things. It was a bit difficult training myself to wake up at 5 o'clock every morning, but then again Reg had to be awake early with me, and after a while I soon got the hang of it.

I had three buildings to supervise every day at first, one was the R.A.C. in Croydon and two others. These were all very large buildings and took a lot of looking after. I had to make sure there were staff for all the floors and everyone had arrived for work. If someone hadn't turned up, I would try to persuade one of the other workers to do two floors, with extra money of course.

During the summer holidays some of the lady cleaners would take their children with them and get them to help them in which case they would be quite willing to take on another floor.

One Sunday I took my son with me to the R.A.C. building because they wanted their canteen to have a thorough clean. All the Rexene chairs, about a hundred which were filthy, had to come up like new. Reg was working that day, that was why I decided Tony and I could earn some extra money. The cleaning fluid was supposed to be diluted but it was very hard work rubbing away at each chair and I thought this is going to take more than one Sunday to complete until I accidentally spilled a little of the cleaning fluid on one of the chairs. To my amazement the spot where the liquid fell came clean before my eyes so all we had to do was put the neat liquid on then wipe it off with clean water. The hardest part of the job was running to get clean water to wipe the chairs off.

There was a cleaning supervisor for each building, who also had an eye on things, but I made a point of examining every building thoroughly once a month. Every morning I had to ring into head office from whichever building I went to first to let them know I wasn't late - even supervisors were checked on, and my starting time was 6 o'clock. I would go home at 8 o'clock to wake Tony, give him his breakfast and take him to school, he was about eleven years old then.

I used to go into the office to make my report and then I would pick up materials used for cleaning and deliver them to the various offices ready for the next morning. Many's the time when I would have to set-to myself to do some cleaning including toilets (not just one set but six) on each floor because we would be short of staff. I am afraid that cleaning staff who worked on a casual basis only got paid for the amount of work they did and weren't very conscientious and if they didn't feel like coming to work, they just didn't bother.

Fridays were a nightmare because I had to go and find all the cleaners to give them their wages, every building, every floor, sometimes I would yell out when I couldn't find anyone. I must have walked for miles on my Friday rounds. I had to see the office manager once a week to see if there had been any complaints regarding the cleaning being done satisfactorily.

My hours were 6 o'clock to 12 o'clock but often I didn't get home until 1.30. I kept getting another building added to my list so that in the finish I had six, unfortunately three of them were not in Croydon but some distance away and having all this responsibility was beginning to tell on me. I would go home and collapse onto the settee and fall asleep. I wondered after a while if this was the job for me.

I had not been feeling very well for some time so decided to see my doctor and ask her for a tonic. Dr. Reynolds was a very good doctor and I looked upon her as a friend. Her son used to come and play with my son when he wasn't at school. We both moved into our houses at the same time and her house was right opposite mine.

She told me after an examination that I would have to go to see a specialist immediately and promptly got onto the telephone herself and made an appointment for me at King's College Hospital for the very next day. I hadn't expected anything like this to happen but then, when the doctor told me I had fibroids which needed to come out quickly, I thought back and remembered that my tummy had swollen up lately and I was also having difficulty passing water, apart from feeling unwell in general.

The doctor wanted me to go into hospital for the hysterectomy operation that same weekend but I told him that I couldn't because my daughter Ann was having a baby and it was due any day. I had promised to go and look after her when she came home. In those days when you had a baby you only went into the hospital for the birth so that was why I wanted to take care of her for a week. The doctor told me to phone the hospital as soon as possible to arrange to be admitted.

The following week it was snowing, it was the end of November and Duncan, Ann's husband, phoned me to say that she had just gone into hospital to have her baby. She lived in Colchester and we lived in London in the Crystal Palace area. The radio was asking people to keep off the roads because of the heavy snowfall but nothing was going to keep me away from Ann when she needed me, so my son Tony and I started out taking with us sacks and a spade in case we got caught in a drift.

I was really surprised when we seemed to have the roads to ourselves. Lorries were parked along the way covered in snow, but Tony and I just carried on at a steady 20 miles an hour. We had left very early in the morning so there was not much traffic about. We arrived at Ann's just as it began to snow again. She opened the door and fell into my arms crying, she didn't think that I would be coming in such bad weather.

She had a lovely baby boy. He was beautiful, but then he was my first grandchild. I stayed for the week then I told Ann I had to have an operation.

CHAPTER 20
I Do a Variety of Interesting Jobs

I didn't tell her what sort of operation because I didn't want her to worry after just having a baby, so when Tony and I arrived home I phoned the hospital and made arrangements to go in the following weekend.

Reg took me to hospital, the sister asked Reg to sign a consent form, being the next of kin, as the operation was a serious one. His face went grey because I hadn't told him that it would be so bad. I know that he can't stand any thought of blood or pain or hospitals, just to go into a hospital made him feel ill.

I remember when I had Ann, I was sitting up in hospital as pleased as punch with my baby, Reg came in and nearly fainted and that was when I wasn't even ill. I told him not to come and see me immediately after the operation because I would be asleep recovering from the anaesthetic. I didn't want him to be upset seeing me with tubes and a drip etc.

I had the operation the following day. I was only half awake when I realised Reg was sitting holding my hand, my brother-in-law Arthur had brought him in to see me. I wish he hadn't because Reg passed out and the nurses had to look after him. The pain, I shall never forget the pain.

They fixed a tube into my stomach into which they put a drug called Curare to ease the pain. Apparently, this was a new idea so they asked me for my permission to use it. I said that I didn't care what they did as long as they took away the pain, which it did, but it didn't last long and I was soon crying out for them to do it again as the relief was wonderful and I could doze off.

They were only allowed to give me so much because Curare is a poison and too much would have killed me, so I had to bear much pain before I got better. The sister was very kind and looked after me herself quite a lot. She would sit and talk to me and one time I told her about a dream I had had whilst I was asleep. I was lying on the top of a cliff, the sun was shining very brightly and the grass was warm and comfortable. I was happy and felt as if I wanted to stay there and just go to sleep but the sun was too bright and then I woke up. The dream seemed to last for quite a long time and I still remember it well.

After about a week I was allowed to get up and have a bath, a nurse wheeled me down and stayed with me helping me to wash. Whilst in the bath I saw a lot of bruising around my heart and asked the nurse, who was only a youngster, how I had got them. Then she said that my heart had stopped for three minutes whilst having the operation. I confirmed this by reading my chart, so I guess I am lucky to be here, God hadn't wanted me just yet.

After I had been in hospital for two weeks, I was still very weak and sore, they wanted to send me away for another two weeks, but all I wanted to do was go home. Reg had two weeks off to look after me and, besides, he couldn't stand not having me at home and I missed him so much. After six weeks I was ready to start work again. I wasn't really fit enough to work full time and no way was I going back to being a cleaning supervisor. That is one of the worst possible jobs anyone can do, so I decided to go back into catering where I could do as much or as little as I wanted by working casually.

Mum was pleased because it meant that she could have me to pick her up and take her home, no more waiting for trains and buses. I found it a great help having a car because some of the jobs didn't finish until after midnight.

Let me tell you some of my experiences which stick in my mind. I regularly went to Lambeth Palace when they had their functions and, by now, I was very experienced and looked neat and tidy, my hair was auburn and I wore it in big fat curls most of the time to keep it off my shoulders. I was also quite a trim 9 stones, the uniform I wore for the particular caterer who did Lambeth Palace functions was a black dress with a pink bib and brace pinafore. I used to wait on top table and serve Dr. Ramsey. He was a lovely man and it was a pleasure to serve him. I used to hide a bottle of wine behind the high curtain at the back so that I could top up the glasses for the top table. Dr Ramsey didn't drink much but he didn't like to see his glass empty. You know I loved that man, he was just as charming to us waiters and waitresses as he was to Royalty, a real man of the people and a man of God.

I told you about the time when Mum and I got a £5 note each for what we thought was a disastrous reception, well this account of a wedding at Chelsea Town Hall was exactly the opposite. I was in charge and it was to be a very special occasion with no expense spared. The hall was full of wonderful flowers, it wasn't a sit- down wedding, a buffet and champagne with a large band playing. It was a top hat and tails wedding, the bride and bridesmaids wore gorgeous dresses, all the guests were beautifully attired, they had everything and our staff really did themselves proud in making everything go smoothly.

Came the time to leave, the best man gave me a cheque to cover the bill, then gave me two pounds, yes two pounds, to share between six of us. We had six shillings and eight pence each. He had turned and gone before I had the chance to give it back to him. It's a good job the girls knew me otherwise they would have thought that I was keeping the tip for myself as some managers do.

Another wedding we did turned out like one that was in the Bible. Everyone arrived for the wedding reception, we had everything ready, the tables looked lovely with the flowers and the wedding cake in place. The hall we were in was in Wandsworth. The happy couple had only arrived a few minutes when all the other guests came. Suddenly there was an almighty row, everybody was shouting and pushing and shoving, we didn't know what to do. I told the rest of the girls to go in the kitchen and keep well out of the way, we had never had this happen at a wedding before.

All of a sudden it became very quiet, we went out into the hall to find that all the bridegroom's family, including the bridegroom, had gone. The father of the bride came up to me and said "It's a shame to waste all this food, will your girls go out into the street and bring in some people to share it with us, it's cost me enough?" So, some of the family and some of the girls went out and brought back enough people to fill the seats. There were old ladies with their shopping trolleys, quite a few of them, some young couples, a lady with a little boy, and many more. I never did find out what it was all about, but anyway all the food was eaten, and enjoyed.

Once a year the Lyceum dance hall in the strand held the Miss World Contest. Mum and I were usually picked to attend at the Cafe De Paris after the contest when the contestants and their chaperons would have a dinner and dance. This particular year, my Ann asked me if I could get a programme with signatures of the famous people and Miss World, so not wanting to let her down, I decided to do the best I could.

This year Mum couldn't come, she was doing another job so I went alone. I took with me a long dress to change into out of my black dress, white apron and collar (the caterer who did this job had his waitresses in black and white). I waited on Joe Loss's table this year, he always played at this function. I was pleased because he gave me a good tip.

After we had finished serving and had cleared up, we got paid and had to leave immediately, I took my things and changed in the ladies' cloakroom keeping out of sight until all the staff had left. It was great. I went around collecting dozens of autographs, I saw Peter Sellers and headed for him, he asked me to sit down, put his arm around my shoulders giggling (he had imbibed the wine a little). I told him who I was and without hesitation he signed my card and said "Have you got Johnnie's yet?" I said "No". Then he promptly stood up and called out loudly across the room "Hey, Johnnie" (he had to call loudly because the band was playing and there was a lot of joyous noise going on) and John Mills came over, signed the card, gave me a kiss on the cheek, then took me to another part of the room where his daughter Hayley was sitting, so I got her signature too. My card was full, it was time to leave, I had to leave by the main entrance where the manager of the Cafe De Paris and the commissioner were. I held my head up high, said goodnight and they gave me a box of chocolates, all enclosed in a lovely tapestry box.

This was a lovely night to remember. Ann was well pleased with her present especially the box of chocolates. She kept the tapestry box for some time - I wonder what happened to it.

Dickie Attenborough and his wife Sheila Simms were having a housewarming party. They had bought a lovely house in one of the London Squares and had invited just about everyone in the entertainment business to come. There were stage, screen and radio stars and stars from the television, just mention a name and they were there.

I was to take a party of our girls to hand out drinks and champagne. We didn't know what to expect when we got to the house, what we didn't expect was for it to be empty of furniture, carpets, and curtains. It was a completely empty house. Not for long though because it was soon overflowing with people. I went from floor to floor picking out the stars that I knew, there were so many that I lost count after 70.

ZaZa Gabor came, flashing all her jewellery and calling everyone 'darling', even me. I saw a young girl of about fifteen sitting on the floor in the corner of one of the rooms. I asked her who she was with and she said "I'm with mummy, ZaZa Gabor". She was such a plain little thing and not a bit like her mother. Jesse Matthews was very well known. I had admired her, especially for her dancing, since I was a young girl, so I made a point of meeting her and was rather surprised at how tall and buxom she was. I'm only 5ft 3" tall and I had to look up to talk to her. Shirley Bassey was another favourite of mine, she was very flamboyant and exciting. As a matter of fact, I got so carried away with meeting so many personalities that I did something I would never do normally. I went out onto the

154

balcony upstairs, there was a huge crowd outside watching all the stars arrive and cheering as they recognised each one, the police were out in force holding them back, I took off my apron and regally waved to the crowd, who cheered and waved back. I wonder who they think they were waving to, not a waitress acting the fool I'll be bound.

I was doing quite a bit of work for Graison Caterers, they used to do a fair bit of catering for the better class. There were the livery halls like Millers, Carpenters, Fishmongers, etc. Some of the halls had weekly lunches which Graisons did regularly. The tables would look a treat all with shining silverware and the beautiful flowers.

I have done many cocktail parties etc. at which royalty, including the Queen and the Duke of Edinburgh, Princess Margaret, Princess Ann and the dear Queen Mother attended. I have attended the Queen Mother quite a few times, she has always been charming. One time that sticks in my mind was when there was a dinner presentation to honour Dame Margot Fonteyn, she was to be presented with a medal, I believe. Dame Margot was beautiful, she was a ballet dancer. She had brought her husband who was paralysed. I was on the top table looking after the Queen Mother together with a church dignitary and Dame Margot and her husband. Dame Margot cut up her husband's food and with loving patience fed him.

I noticed that the Queen Mother had lipstick on her little finger where she had applied her lipstick, it somehow made her seem more loveable. She was always that, she used to seek out the waitress's room so that she could wave goodbye and thank us, no other Royal ever does that, it made our day somehow. It will be a great loss when she is no longer with us, she had the job thrust onto her and did it right regally.

CHAPTER 21
The Day I Danced with Ringo Starr at Chelsea Town hall

After a few years of just doing casual work I was asked by
Mr. Grainger, the boss of Graison Caterers, whilst doing a
dinner at his banqueting suite in Forest Hill, if I knew
anyone who could do office work, so of course I said "Yes,
I could". He offered me a part-time job doing bookkeeping
three times a week, the offices were in Victoria in the heart
of London, so I started another part of my career.

Working in the office I came into contact with quite a few
of the customers and after a while I was introduced to them
saying that I would be the hostess when they had their
dinner dance etc. at Forest Hill. I had been made hostess
and was to run the Galleon bar which was a small bar used
as a reception bar for the guests when they arrived. I was
working every other day in the office but also doing dinner-
dances, weddings etc. at Forest Hill banqueting suite.

I could write a book about the functions that I have attended
but I shall only tell about a few that linger in my mind.

As I type this, I have just heard that Leslie Crowther, that
dear man, has just died. This brings to mind the time he
came to the banqueting suite to do a cabaret. I had always
admired Leslie, he came into the reception bar for a drink
after all the guests were seated having dinner. I gave him a

drink and he gave me a kiss. We chatted for a while when he told me that I reminded him of his wife Jean. She had the same colour hair as me so I guess that was why he spent the next half hour talking about his wife and children. I should have been working but I was enthralled. At the end of the evening, when I might add, he was a big success, he came looking for me, and in front of the other girls gave me a hug and a kiss goodbye. I never forgot that, every time I saw him on the box afterwards, I remembered that evening.

Sometimes coming home in the early hours of the morning after working, I would be stopped by the police who would ask where I was going, where I had been etc. One particular night, I had just done a wedding, it wasn't late, about 10 0'clock, I stopped by the jellied eel stall, I just fancied some. I parked the car on double yellow lines right beside the stall, there was nothing about but two policemen who I hadn't seen, who were standing in the shop doorway. On returning to the car they were waiting for me. I laughed, told them where I had been and offered them one of my jellied eels, they laughed and took one and told me to buzz off.

I used to do quite a lot of jobs at the Guildhall in London. One night, or should I say early morning, we were coming home after doing the Lord Mayor's Banquet, there wasn't a soul about, I had three other girls in the car who I was giving a lift to, when I went through a red light. I wasn't speeding and there was absolutely no danger because it wasn't a cross road, only one turning coming out on my right but coming out on my right was also a police car which promptly overtook me and made me stop.

The policeman got out, I wound down my window and he very sternly asked me where we had been, had we been drinking? I told him that we had just finished working at the Guildhall (we used to give some food and a drink to any police that just happened to come by) so I said "Hey, I recognise you, didn't I give you a drink at the Guildhall earlier on? He laughed and said "Yes". He started chatting but I said we had better get going as we were tired and had had a busy night. I had never seen that Policeman in my life, but I never got a ticket. I think that the police are wonderful, many's the time they have been helpful to me.

Sometimes I would have to take some extra wine or spirits from the office to a job in London where they had run out, or perhaps the van hadn't delivered it. There was no way I could carry the stuff myself and that meant that I would have to park on yellow lines or in a restricted area. There always seemed to be a lot of policemen about in those days and I had no hesitation of asking one to keep an eye on my car whilst I got a porter to carry the drink inside. I wasn't ever refused assistance they just said "don't be long" or "make it quick".

I remember another time Mum and I went to do a Jewish wedding, we had to be there at eight thirty in the morning because there was a lot of preparing to do. Jewish weddings are the most extravagant that you could possibly attend. The lady we would be working for had been in a concentration camp during the war, she had her number burnt into her arm, she never talked about it but we knew. I had done numerous jobs for her so she put me on the top table because she trusted my ability. We worked really hard preparing the food, also there was a little man in the kitchen walking around watching everything we did whilst we prepared this great feast. You see, you weren't allowed to mix the meat with the milk, all the utensils and the sinks had to be kept completely apart.

They had a buffet that was fit for a king to start with, then later on they sat down to a six- course meal, but that's not all, after a few hours they were served coffee and cake. The ladies all looked wonderful, their hair styles were magnificent (I discovered later that they all wore wigs). It seems that when these Jewish ladies got married, they had to have all their hair shaved off, because it was thought unclean. The men on the other hand wore their hair long. They had beards and strands of hair around their faces, even the young boys had corkscrew twists of hair around their faces.

They have a wonderful way of getting married, they don't get married in church, they get married in the courtyard under a canopy in the eyes of God then afterwards they break a mirror, which means they will not forsake each other ever. At one of the Jewish weddings I attended we were so short of staff that we were rushed off our feet all day, we couldn't contact any staff that weren't already working so I suggested my daughter Ann should come along.

She was only fourteen but it would be another pair of hands, so I phoned Ann and explained to her how to get to North London and which station to get off where I would meet her. She arrived in time to serve the main meal.

I was on the top table, so I put her on the table close to me which had the nearest relatives and told them of our dilemma. I told them that she had never done anything like it before but was willing to help. They were very kind and said that they would make it as easy as possible for her, and with my help in between, the party went with a swing. In fact, I think that Ann's table was the happiest in the room, there was a great deal of laughter when she made a small mistake, and everyone took it in good part.

At the end of the meal it is customary to give your waitress a tip. Ann had twice as much from her table as I did from mine, she also got a full day's wages for coming to help out. In the end she took home more wages than I did. She was tired, but very happy. The other girls didn't mind at all that she had the same wages as the rest of us, it meant that there was an extra pair of hands to help with the clearing up. It didn't matter that we had been there for fourteen hours and she had only been there for five.

That wedding reminds me of a bible story, when the man who owned the vineyard paid everyone the same amount, the men who came in first thing in the morning and the men who came in for the last hour. The earlier workers said they were being unfairly treated. Not so with Ann, everyone liked her and said that they hoped they would see her again. Ann did come with me sometimes to earn herself some pocket money. I taught her, just as Mum taught me.

Italian weddings are something else, they are a very noisy and boisterous affair with everyone talking at once and most often in their own language. There is so much noise that it is a relief to get back into the kitchen. One of their customs is to give sugared almonds to all the lady guests, these sweeties are put into muslin bags and tied with ribbon then placed where each lady will be sitting. I liked Italian weddings (apart from the noise), they were always so polite, every one that I have done has been a very happy affair. I have also done some millionaires' weddings and parties.

I remember one that I did, we were picked up by coach and taken on a long ride into the country. The drive up to the mansion was about a mile long (or so it seemed). They had great marquees which were all lined with pleated satin, there were chandeliers hanging from the top and wooden floors covered with carpet. There wasn't just one marquee but three, one was for a dining area, one was for dancing and the other for toilets and rest rooms. There was even a covered walkway from the house to the marquees so that if it rained people wouldn't get wet.

When we had finished laying-up, we had to get ourselves spruced up to be examined by the lady (who really was a Lady) to see if we were good enough and neat enough, then we had a little time to ourselves. Some of the girls wandered through the large gardens which, by the way, were lit up by coloured lights placed strategically in the shrubs, a lovely sight to see. Me, I sneaked a look around the house which was like a fairy story. I wonder how many servants they employed to keep a house that size clean, I would have loved to work in a house like that. When I look back to when I did cleaning for those miserable people who made me work like a slave, it makes you think that even servants can have a better class of living.

Getting back to the party, there were about four hundred guests, there were five serving areas, waiters and waitresses, everything was so well planned that nobody had to wait long to be served. I remember there was a large band. I don't remember who it was but it must have been well-known.
Max Bygraves was one of the entertainers, unfortunately I didn't hear him because by that time we had finished serving and were getting ready to be taken back in the coach to London.

I have been a waitress in hundreds of places, these are a few that I did regularly, The Star and Garter Home, Richmond, Temple Bowling, Herne Hill, Morden College, Blackheath, Knightsbridge Barracks, Hyde Park, Penge Conservative

Club, Dulwich Conservative Club, Archbishop Amigo, Camberwell (where Ann had her wedding), John Marshall, various weddings of all denominations, The Guildhall, The Palaces, including Lambeth Palace, most of the livery halls and lots of private dinner parties and cocktail parties.

Sometimes Mr Graison had so many jobs on that he would run out of casual chefs so I would fill in by going to the smaller dinners. One I did was for a well-known newspaper magnet. It was only for eight people and four courses. He was so pleased that he came down to the kitchen to thank me in the way that is most appreciated, of course, the tip. Sometimes I had so much work especially over Christmas when I would have two or sometimes three jobs in one day, no wonder I kept slim.
I worked at the Livery Hall, called Sadlers, (the hall for saddle makers and horse equipment) for eight weeks. I only went there once a week to cook lunches for 12 men who were directors etc. The Bursar's wife, who usually did the cooking, was in hospital having a serious operation. I was serving lunch there one day when the Bursar asked me if I could fill in and do the cooking. I told him that I had some experience in cooking for private dinner parties so he asked me to go along the following week to cook, then he would see if I would do. This I did and went along for the next eight weeks.

It was very pleasant. The Bursar would give me a drink whilst I was cooking, he also gave me a packet of cigarettes. Christmas was coming when I left. The

164

Directors bought me gifts of bottles of wine and chocolates and thanked me for all that I had done. I quite enjoyed it, I have always liked cooking.

My boss, Mr. Grainger, always had me to his house to do the cooking when he had a dinner party or birthday party. I didn't keep hidden away in the kitchen all the time. After a few years I knew all the guests by name and they knew me as Margaret and used to come out into the kitchen sometimes to have a chat.

We had some great parties at his house, one time he had a fancy- dress party so I borrowed a Brownie's uniform (I didn't tell him I was going to dress up. I never wore a uniform or apron when I worked in his house). It was a great laugh especially when one of his friends came dressed as a boy scout, they just had to take a photograph of us acting the fool together.

Another time that comes to mind was when his son was having his 21st birthday party. There were five of us working at the party. We were all given a drink but one of the girls imbibed a little too much so when everyone changed into their costumes to go swimming (yes, he had a large swimming pool in the garden with changing chalets as well), she stripped off down to her pants and bra and dived in, nobody minded, she was no girl, she must have been at least sixty years old then and had worked for our boss for at least 20 years.

Mrs. Grainger was a lovely person, she worked as well, one of her jobs was to make the flower arrangements. Sometimes there were so many to be made that I would help her. One time my boss was asked by Mecca to lend them three girls for their Bali Hai Club in Streatham, just for three evenings, as none of his waitresses had turned up. So, Mum and I and another girl volunteered to go along.

The Club was situated right over the top of the ice rink, you could see the skaters through big glass windows all along one side in the part which was made into a small restaurant. The place was decorated as a south sea island with nets hanging from the ceiling and all sorts of shells and ornaments suitable to lend atmosphere. We girls had to wear brightly coloured dresses as a sort of uniform which were made for us. We only went there for three evenings but it continued for four years. It was a small club with a disc jockey for the music and two small dance floors, one each end, not suitable for ballroom dancing but ideal for disco or smooching. The place used to get crowded from 9 o'clock to 1 o'clock in the morning. Most people, who had to be members by the way, liked to have the same waitress to look after them all evening, and Mum and I always had our own little groups and odd couples to see to.

We did very well for tips, in fact we made more in tips than we got for our wages. Some of the members were questionable, and we used to hear all sorts of things which we would never repeat or discuss with anyone, most were young men. One instance which is worth repeating was a time when two of these lads stole a lorry from a service station on the motorway and it turned out that it was full of sausage skins. There was no way anyone would buy that from them and they did feel silly.

There was always one man about 35 years old who always stood in the same place at the end of the bar, the barman used to give him his drinks and he tipped him well for looking after him. He was the man who would buy any goods available. No one knew his name or where he came from and although he never ordered a drink from us waitresses, he used to tip us because he wasn't supposed to be served at the bar because it was waitress service only.

It was really hard work rushing through the crowd with a tray full of drinks. If you spilt one you had to pay for it yourself or one of your boys paid for it for you.

We closed at 1 o'clock but by the time we had cleared up it was about 2 o'clock before we got away. I had bought a new car, my first new car. It was a Ford Anglia, a nice red colour and I had only had it a couple of weeks when it was stolen. I had been brushing it out and cleaning it when I noticed that it was getting late, so I put the ashpan and brush in the back on the floor and got ready to go to work at the Bali Hai.

It was a Friday night and when I came out to go home in the early hours of the morning my car had gone - I always left it in the Bali Hai car park and there was nothing there.

I was in a panic, the manager gave me a lift home and the next night I told the man at the bar that my car had been stolen. He was very kind and said "Don't worry", he would see what he could do. I gave him the details and he gave me a £10 note to get a taxi home each night (I was only getting £3.50 a night wages).

I had informed the police but I was still very surprised when a policeman turned up on our doorstep three days later to say that they had had a phone call to say that my car was found a few streets away, was I pleased!

When I went to pick up the car it had been carefully cleaned and no damage had been done. I went to work the following night and the man at the bar said "Have you got your car back?" I said Yes, thank you very much". He said "Was it OK?" and of course I told him all about it. I never thought I would be glad to know someone like him.

There were some bad times at the club, sometimes things got out of hand and a fight would develop. We girls would disappear into our room, there were five of us and we would bolt the door. One time the noise was really bad, glasses breaking, chairs being thrown, girls screaming, shouting and general bedlam, there was a banging on our door and someone saying "Please let me in, I'm hurt". We saw a young man who was bleeding badly, he had severed his artery in the crook of his arm. When I opened his arm to stop the flow, the blood spurted up to the ceiling and all over the walls. I held my fingers on the cut until we could get help. He had been cut with flying glass and was in no way connected with the row that was going on. The fight only lasted about 10 minutes until the police arrived and it was the first bad incident in three years.

Most of the people came to enjoy themselves and were ordinary respectable young folk who just enjoyed the disco and dancing. The worst part of working at the Bali Hai was that we had to work every Christmas eve and New Year's eve, not once did we have one off. I was supposed to have a Christmas eve off. I had been promised it because we were going to have a lot of visitors but at 9 o'clock I got a phone call to go to work because some of the girls hadn't turned up and I was told that if I didn't go I needn't bother to come back again ever, so I went to work and earned so much in tips and presents from my regulars that I didn't mind so much after all.

Mum was still working with me and she really looked forward to going to work there, her boys were really nice to her and she was happy. They would buy her a gin and tonic and after a couple (which she had to drink on the quiet because we weren't allowed to drink on duty) she had a happy face for the whole evening.

As I have said, we stayed there for 4 years but the end came with another fight. It started so suddenly, someone threw a chair at the bar, then all hell broke loose. We girls tried to make for our room, I was trapped at the wrong end of the bar so I hid behind a pillar until I could get away. I was really frightened. Two of the boys protected me until I could get to safety. Where was Mum? She wasn't there, I came out again avoiding flying debris, then I found her lying on the floor smothered in blood. My God, was she all right? Some of the boys carried her to our room. She was all right, the blood wasn't hers. Our Manager though had been hurt and was bleeding to death with a stab wound in his bottom. He had gone to break up a fight and had got stabbed for his trouble.

That was the end, we never wanted to see anything like that again. The place was a wreck and we never went back.

Shortly after the Bali Hai incident, I was sent to do a job at Chelsea Town Hall, this was to be a promotion of the record by John Lennon (a member of the Beatles group), the song was called "Give Peace a Chance". There were about a thousand guests, most of them teenagers, we served only Champagne and fruit juice, all the time there was the record playing loudly over and over again.

The youngsters were dancing to the music. Ringo Starr, who was the Beatles' drummer, came with his entourage, his wife, manager and a few others. It was extremely hot and I was thirsty, so I asked one of the waitresses to bring me a cold drink of orange. When it came in a half pint glass, I drowned the lot in one go. A little later I knew that there was more than orange juice in the glass, most of it had been Champagne. I never ever drink whilst working and if I do drink it is only the odd one at weddings etc.

I was very merry, made my way over to Ringo and said
"Why aren't you dancing Ringo?" He said "Because I have
no one to dance with". I said "I'll dance with you" and
promptly handed my tray of drinks to his manager, took
him by the hand and lead him to the centre of the floor. We
danced and, as we danced, the crowd formed a big circle
round us clapping their hands in tune with "Give Peace A
Chance". I was having a wonderful time. I was high on
drink and flung myself with abandon into the dance.

The reporters appeared and began flashing their lights and
taking photos. I would have loved to have got hold of some
of those photographs, me dancing with Ringo Starr in my
pink pinny.
When the music stopped Ringo took me by the hand, back
to his wife, he kissed me on the cheek and said that he had
enjoyed that, then he signed one of the records for me. I
said that "It's not much use to me, I have two children, they
will be fighting over it", so he said "Never mind, I will give
you another one" and he did. I was amazed at myself for
what I had done. I was in charge of the job, I wondered
what the other waitresses would think and what if it got
back to my boss. I needn't have worried though, they had
all been watching and thoroughly enjoying themselves. I
was never found out. Ann and Tony still have the records,
both are in mint condition still in the wrapper they came in.

CHAPTER 22
My only Granddaughter Emma is Born

Ann had had another baby, a little girl named Emma. Two beautiful children, John my grandson watched out for Emma, he always knew what she wanted, she was late learning to talk because John would talk for her, how he understood her chatter I never knew. If she wanted something, she would chatter to John who would then tell his mummy what she had said. He was always sticking up for her when she was naughty. He would share his sweets while she would save hers until she went to bed, putting the wrappers under the bed. Mind you, she was only a tiny tot.

I haven't said too much about the family because this autobiography is being written for them to understand where they came from and after all they know their own life story. I wish that I had known all about my grandparents and their grandparents etc.

Tony was doing well in school. He had passed his examinations and could have gone to Dulwich College on a free pass but because he lived out of the area he wasn't allowed to. We were all so disappointed. He ended up eventually at Stanley Technical School, which was the same school his Dad went to.

Tony did really well and worked hard, he made new friends. One of his friends called George was brilliant, without much effort he always came top in everything. Tony tried to beat him and studied really hard. He could never beat him but he always followed closely behind. Tony went to University, King's College, in the heart of London. He steadily progressed to getting his degree, we were so proud.

When Tony was 21, he decided he wanted a birthday party at home with all his friends to come in fancy dress. I dressed him up in a skirt and blouse, stockings and high heeled shoes, a wig and jewellery. I bought a record of "The Stripper" and then he practiced doing a striptease before his friends came for the party. It was a great party, as usual not the usual party fare but a huge pot of curry with rice, steak and kidney pie, sausages with baked potatoes in their jackets, bread pudding (I couldn't leave out the bread pudding, that was a favourite of his friends), mountains of French bread and butter, trifle, fruit salad and cake with ice cream and cream cheese and biscuits and lots more. Most of his friends came from University and being away from home they were always hungry.

Came the time for his striptease, it was hilarious, he stripped slowly to the music, flirting with the boys and throwing his clothes in the air. Everybody was falling about laughing, the final part came when all he had on was lacy knickers, or so they thought. He went out of the door just leaving one leg showing and threw his knickers into the room, the boys chased him upstairs where they found he had his swimming trunks on. It was a great party, one of my fondest memories.

Shortly after Tony left home, he had got a job at Sellafield which is in the Lake District, over three hundred miles away. It was very quiet at home now Tony had gone. He couldn't come all that way home very often and it was so far away that we couldn't go to see him very much either. I missed the bustle of having a son at home, I missed his friends coming round, I missed the parties, but most of all I missed the times we played together. After dinner in the evenings, we often had a game of Chess or Back Gammon or cards, we played for a million pounds a game. Of course, no money changed hands, it was just fun. Even when Tony was going out, he still found time to give me a few games.

Just Reg and me left at home now. Ann was now living up at Whitby, North Yorkshire. What I missed most, because they ended up so far away from us, was seeing the grandchildren grow up. I would have loved it if they had lived just round the corner and popped in for tea to see their Nan, or I could have taken them out to the park, or swimming or to the circus, just to baby sit or the hundred and one other things that doting grandparents do. We only managed to see them a few times a year, thank God for the telephone.

CHAPTER 23
My Son Marries

Tony had left university where he had done very well and
had got himself a job at Sellafield in Cumbria. It didn't take
him very long to get himself noticed and he was gradually
climbing the ladder to success. He had bought a miner's
cottage very cheap and with the help of his friends and a
builder they made it into a little warm, comfortable home,
of course with a little help from his mum and dad as well.
Tony had girlfriends, but it wasn't until he met Heather, a
Scottish lassie, that an engagement was announced. They
were to be married in August in Scotland. It was a long
way to go so Reg and I decided that we would fly there.
We took Reg's sister with us. Tony's London friends hired
a mini bus to bring them and we all stayed in the same hotel
where the wedding reception was going to be. Ann and
Duncan drove up from Bristol, Emma was a bridesmaid and
John was an usher. It was really funny on the wedding day.
There was I standing in my slip ironing our wedding
clothes with all the boys bringing their shirts along for me
to freshen up. The hotel was very good, they loaned us an
ironing board and iron and brought it up to our room. Just
imagine me standing with my hair in curlers with the boys
sitting on the bed chatting and laughing waiting for their
shirts. Reg's sister is very superstitious and can't bear any
artificial flowers in the house. The first thing she did when
she got to her room was to throw the artificial flowers she

175

found there out of the window. They were still there when we left the next day.

The wedding was a great success, everything went off beautifully. Tony and Heather left to spend their honeymoon, two weeks in St. Lucia. A far cry from our honeymoon which was a week in Hastings, and that was nearly cancelled because the hotel we had booked had changed hands and was being renovated. Still, Reg and I would have been happy anywhere, it doesn't really matter where you are when you are with the person you love.

Tony and Heather's Wedding

It was a long way to go when we went to visit Tony and Heather, over three hundred miles, so once again we couldn't see them very often. It was wonderful when we did get to see them especially when Iain, the first baby, arrived. He was so beautiful, just like his mum and dad. Then after a while came Stephen another beautiful son. Their family is now complete and they have moved to Knutsford near Manchester, which is only 160 miles away. Now we can see each other more often, especially now that Reg and I have both retired. Instead of trying to fix a weekend away we can now go for a whole week. We have also been able to share holidays with them which gives us a chance to know the children and love them more.

Tony and Heather at Stephen's Christening

CHAPTER 24
My Last Job Working for a Printer

My boss decided he wanted to retire when he had a good offer from one of the big companies. They offered me a job with them but I didn't want to work for a big company. I was always happiest in a small firm, so I started looking for another job. I got myself a job with a scaffolding firm. There were only two of us in the office, myself and a young girl of about 21, I was 50 by this time. There wasn't too much office work to do, just the books and wages, V.A.T. returns, Inland Revenue, Tax, filing, the usual jobs, but most of all I had to talk to the scaffolders who were not paid a weekly wage, they were paid for what they did.

We had to deliver the scaffolding equipment to them so that they could get on with the job. Sometimes the materials just didn't turn up on time for them to get on. They would be on the phone to me using the most awful language, blaming me in no uncertain terms, threatening to sort me out. It was nothing to do with me that the gear hadn't been delivered on time. The two bosses who were partners used to arrange all the transport. They were mostly a rough uncouth lot with few exceptions. I put up with it for a few months because the pay was good but then I just had to leave. I started looking in the papers for another job.

This was a difficult time, I had not had many jobs and it is very hard to find a new job when you have worked for years quite happily. The first job I phoned for was at Thornton Heath, a printers who wanted a fully qualified bookkeeper, which I now was. I phoned up for an appointment and they asked me if I could go along the next day. I said that I was working, would they see me after 5 o'clock? They agreed, so along I went, they hadn't asked me how old I was so I wasn't sure how I would get on.

There were four people in the office when I arrived, it was hard to tell which one was in charge because they all asked me questions. I must have been there more than an hour. They shook my hand and said that they would let me know on Monday, this was Friday. I said that would suit me because I had another appointment just around the corner. There was another job just around the corner but I hadn't phoned them for an appointment yet. I had only been home 20 minutes when I got a phone call asking me to take the job. This was great, a local job, no more travelling to the City every day, I had made my own terms, four long days a week and Wednesday off. I wanted Wednesday off so that I could do my housework and main shopping so that I could have the weekend free to do as we liked.

In the 10 years that I worked at Jupiter Arts, I had lots of traumatic experiences. They were always in trouble with paying their bills, cash was always hard to come by, the worst of the debtors were the Inland Revenue and V.A.T. I got to know the bailiffs very well, also the local courts became a regular outing for me. You know we had more money owing to us than we owed. Most of the big companies were the ones who were so slow in paying, those who had the most were the least likely to part with it under three months whereas our suppliers needed theirs a lot quicker, hence the courts and bailiffs and tax man who were always after us.

After a few years my boss took a holiday leaving me in charge of the office. He hadn't been on holiday for years, he couldn't remember when. Then, every year after that, when he could see that nothing had gone wrong in his absence, he would take his lovely wife to his thatched cottage in Dorset. He used to loan his cottage to Reg and me, but that's another story.

I was there for 10 years until I was 61. We had put our house up for sale and was looking for a bungalow to live near my daughter and her family. My son would have liked us to live near him, but being Londoners we couldn't face living in the Lake District, it's cold and wet and a bit desolate, so we were looking for a place not too far from Ann.

We came to stay with Ann for some weekends whilst we toured the estate agents, and the rest of the time we had information sent to us regarding property for sale. We picked out some we liked the sound of, then Ann went to see them. After a few weeks, we came down to see four more bungalows, they were very nice but not for us, so we went back to the agents who said that they had just had someone bring in a bungalow in Nailsea, it hadn't even been photographed yet or advertised.

Reg was fed up, Ann was with us, so Reg sat in the car and refused to come and have a look. As soon as we entered, I knew. I looked at Ann, she looked at me and grinned. We had a quick look round then Ann went and got her dad. We had found our new home. We paid the full asking price because we didn't want to lose it. Mr. and Mrs, Wilson couldn't believe their luck, they had only given it to the estate agents that same morning.

We already had a buyer for our house, so it was just a matter of going through the usual procedures.
When it was time for us to move, my boss and his wife took Reg and me out for a lovely meal where his wife asked me to stay for just another two weeks so that they could have one more holiday before I left, but we were moving to Nailsea in North Somerset in two weeks time so it was out of the question.

We had two weeks to get packed up and after living in our house for 31 years there was a lot of sorting out to do. It was a very busy time because we had so much stuff up in the loft and also we couldn't take all the furniture with us as we were moving into a bungalow. I made many trips to the charity shop with my car loaded up with all sorts of useful things which I had kept in case Ann or Tony could find a use for them.

I had just finished loading up again for a trip to the charity shop one Saturday morning when my next door neighbour's little boy said "Why don't you take it to my school's car boot sale?" So, on the spur of the moment that's what I did. The boot sale was well in progress by the time I arrived so a crowd gathered around as soon as I arrived to see what goodies I had to offer. People were offering money before I had a chance to open the boot. I arrived at ten o'clock and by 11 o'clock I had sold out all but a few things which I gave to the lady on the next stall. I made £60 which in those days was a lot of money. I never asked any money for anything, I just told the people to give me what they wanted.

CHAPTER 25
Retired We Move to Nailsea

On our moving day, the van had left and we were sitting on the floor waiting for the new owners to arrive, they had asked us to stay and give them the key.

Whilst we were waiting I was thinking, we had moved into this house after watching it being built, we had transformed the very large garden into a showpiece, we had brought up two children there and I really expected to be sorry to leave, but I never was. It was time to go, I took one last look at the garden before we left then made our way to Nailsea in the car. The van wasn't going to deliver our furniture until the next day so we went to the bungalow to give it a good clean before we moved in (it wasn't really necessary though, it was spotless). The people moving out had left us a bottle of wine and a note wishing us luck in our new home, I thought that was nice.

Our new next door neighbour came round the day we moved in to introduce himself, and to ask if there was anything he could do to help. We had a little chat and I happened to mention to Reg that we needed an outside tap fitted. I didn't even see this man Cecil go, I turned to Reg and said what a funny man, where did he go? He was back in a little while and the next time I saw him he was lying on his back under the sink fixing up an outside tap. He has been most helpful ever since, we have even given him the keys to our house to look after when we are away. He also waters our greenhouse and garden for us when we are not here. He does loads of jobs for us for which we are most thankful.

My Front Garden in Nailsea

We moved to Nailsea to be near Ann and family, they live only 4 miles away. We are only four miles from Clevedon, four miles from Portishead and 12 miles from Weston-Super-Mare, Wales is only about half an hour's ride away. We are surrounded by the countryside but the most important thing was to live near Ann and the family, how happy can you get?

We had the workmen in for eight weeks making improvements, but we decorated ourselves and made our bungalow into a comfortable home, it's a shame that my

Tony lives so far away, how wonderful it would be if he could live near as well.

Iain, Heather, Tony and Stephen

CHAPTER 26
Miraculous Cure at Alpha Course

I had a lot of time on my hands and now that we had finished working on our bungalow and garden, I needed some other occupation to take up my time.

I found out that the local school had a kindergarten for pre-school children and were looking for volunteers to help, so on the spur of the moment I presented myself and was accepted to work twice a week. I did this for quite a long time and I loved every minute of it, the children also seemed to like me because they would try to always sit next to me, or on my lap. When a small child takes a liking to you there is nothing like it, when they put their hands into yours, or when they want to give you a hug, that's what life is all about. I was most upset when I had to stop going. That is when I developed the trouble with my back.

One day I woke up and couldn't move, something was wrong with my back. I saw the doctor who sent me to see a specialist. I had to wait three months for an appointment when he told me that I needed an operation." I will put you on my list and see you as soon as possible". I was house bound, and in constant pain. I regularly 'phoned the hospital to see if I was going in yet, but nothing happened. After a year of watching for the postman every day, I decided that I would go to the hospital and see the specialist's secretary who I had been talking to.

I don't know how I got there, I was in excruciating pain, the tears where rolling down my cheeks. The secretary looked up her list to see when I was due to go in. "You're not on this year's list" she said, this was June. "We haven't made next year's list out yet". I sobbed my heart out, the girl was so upset to see me so distressed that she said "I will go and talk to the doctor" which she did.
She took me to see him, and he was so kind. He asked if I could afford to pay anything, I said I wasn't insured for an expensive operation, but I could afford something. He told me to ring St.Michael's hospital (which is a private hospital) in Clifton, and ask them how much it would cost to book the operating theatre and two nurses for an hour, and a room for five hours. Then I was to ring him on his mobile to let him know. "Whatever they charge you I will charge the same" he said. We went home, had a sandwich and a cup of tea, then I 'phoned the hospital. One hundred and thirty pounds I was told. I 'phoned the doctor and told him. "Right he said, that's what I will charge you, can you go in tonight". "Of course I can" I said. He said that the hospital would get in touch with me to let me know what time I had to be there. Twenty minutes later, the telephone rang, it was the hospital.

"Can you be here by 5oclock?" "Of course". The time was three o'clock. I rang my daughter at work which is ten miles away to tell her, she left immediately to take me to

St.Michael's. We sat quietly in the car park, holding hands and praying, then we went in. I had no sooner got undressed and in bed when someone came and painted my back with iodine. Five minutes later a porter came to take me to the theatre. I was perfectly calm, I wasn't at all afraid. The doctor had brought his Registrar with him to assist. I had to lie on my tummy with a pillow under me to raise up my back, he told me that he was going to use a long needle with a syringe and insert a liquid into the whole length of my spine. He wanted to tell me what I could feel after each movement, and he was sorry but it would hurt. The nurse held my hands so that I would have something to grip on when I felt the pain. She said a little prayer with me. Please don't worry, just get on and do it as quickly as possible, I have no pain, the Lord is with me-- and He was. Afterwards the doctor told me to rest and take it easy for a few weeks, then I would be perfectly all right. I never felt any pain although I was awake during the whole procedure. The nurse who stood holding my hands talked to me all through it and, although I felt uncomfortable, I wasn't in any pain. The whole thing cost £250. I had been in constant pain for a year and because of the compassion of the doctor I was going to be cured.

It took a few weeks for me to be able to move about very much, but I did so want to go to church. There is a chapel at the end of our road and as soon as I was able, I made my way there one Sunday morning. The people there made me so welcome, I felt at home, so I went back the following

Sunday and the Sunday after that and I have been going
there ever since.

Our church is like one big family, it is a family church with
lots of children and husbands and wives. We all know each
other and look after each other in sickness, especially the
older folk.

I have had my share of illnesses since retiring. I have had
bronchitis, shingles and flu. I have had my gall bladder
removed, my piles and my back trouble. I also had an
accident which resulted in a frozen shoulder which lasted
for two years. When I had the frozen shoulder, our church
was showing the Alpha course which lasted for ten weeks.
Nicky Gumbel is the speaker on these video tapes which
make compulsive viewing, telling about all the wonders of
the Lord, and about His work in the world today. I have
every reason to be a firm believer because of what has
happened to me.

We had just finished discussing what we had been watching
on the video tape about healing when one of our elders put
his hand on my shoulder (the frozen one) and said a prayer
for healing. Everyone had left the room and I sat there for a
moment feeling very hot. When I got up to leave, I was
amazed to find that I could move my arm, I hadn't been able
to move my arm for two years and now I was waving it
about over my head. I ran after David who was the elder
who had touched me. I hugged him and thanked him for
what he had done. He said he had done nothing, the Lord

had used him to transmit his power into me, he had never had anything like that happen to him before. Everyone in our church knew I had a frozen shoulder and were all pleased for me. When I went home Reg thought I had been drinking. There I was waving my arms about. I have been using my arm normally ever since.

CHAPTER 27
The Day I Died

Once more I am due to go for an operation, I remember 25 years ago when I had a Hysterectomy in King's College Hospital. The operation itself was pretty traumatic because I happened to stop breathing during the procedure. This I didn't find out until I went for a bath and noticed the bruising around my heart. The young nurse who was helping me said quite casually "O that is when you died". I began to take notice of what was going on around me. I thought how dismal everyone looked. The ladies looked really seriously ill, but most of them had had their ops and, just like me, were on the road to recovery, so I started making friends with them and persuaded them to comb their hair and put on a little make-up before the doctors' rounds and before visiting time. I borrowed a pair of scissors from one of the nurses to cut off the tangled hair of the old ladies and tied up the remaining hair with ribbons made out of bandages. When the doctors came on their rounds they said "This doesn't look like a hospital with all these lovely ladies looking so blooming" and needless to say the husbands and relatives were highly delighted to see their loved ones looking so much better.

One night when everyone was tucked up in bed ready to sleep, the nurses were sitting on the end of my bed enjoying a glass of sherry, which they were drinking out of medicine glasses (Reg had bought it on the advice from my doctor as a tonic for me) when the Matron arrived. She stood at the end of the bed glowering, the nurses were petrified, I said "Would you like a glass of sherry Matron, it's my birthday and do forgive me for encouraging the nurses to join me?". She said "Thank you very much" and, to the relief of the nurses, she sat on the end of the bed and gossiped with us for a short while. It wasn't my birthday at all!

I stayed in hospital for two weeks and during that time I made myself useful by comforting new incoming patients and doing odd jobs around the ward. (I had been an auxiliary nurse during the last war so I was helping the nurses.

The day I was due to go home was a very moving one for me, the old ladies whose hair I had cut had got their relatives to bring in little presents for 'the hairdresser' and the sister on the ward invited me to her wedding. She said that she wished I was staying a while longer. She was a lovely lady and made my time in hospital an unforgettable experience.

CHAPTER 28
I am Cured of Cancer

Now I am due to go through this traumatic experience again. Let me start at the beginning. I developed Asthma three years ago and since then it has gradually become much worse. I went from a very lively person to a semi invalid and because I was unable to move about very much I naturally started to put on weight, in fact my stomach was ballooning up so much that I went from a size 14 to a size 18 because my dresses would not stretch over my round belly. What I missed most by having this dreadful complaint was the lovely fellowship I have with the members of my church. The old ladies I visited to have a gossip or get their shopping or just to let them know I cared. The toddlers I used to play with on Monday afternoons, we had great fun especially me. Would I ever be back to my old self again? How I missed seeing my son Tony and grandchildren Iain and Stephen who lived in Cumbria and, even when they moved to Knutsford, it was still too far to drive in the state that I was in. The telephone became an essential lifeline.

The breakthrough came when I had some photographs developed that had been in the camera for a year. When I looked at them, I noticed that my stomach was distended so much that it looked as if I was eight months pregnant. I made an appointment with my doctor and told her what I had found. She examined me thoroughly and straight away phoned the hospital for me to have a scan.

I had the scan two days later which shows how urgent it was. In fact, when the doctor who did the scan saw how large the cyst was, she promptly called another doctor to have a look. There was no messing about putting things in the post, straight away she phoned and faxed my doctor who in turn got in touch with the surgeon for an urgent appointment. Within a short time I was in hospital but not before we had some very worrying news. The surgeon said that they were looking for cancer, the dreaded big C. Reg and my family were devastated, there was nothing else we could do. There was only one who could decide and He was the one we turned to. There were at least five churches praying for me, all the prayer groups, and finally a friend of Ann's who lives in California lit a candle for me and got her church to pray on my behalf. I bet the good Lord wondered what was going on, I bet he said "Who is this Margaret?", but he heard and answered our prayers.

I was due to go into hospital on the following Sunday and the previous Tuesday night when I knew that various groups were praying in their own homes, I had the most amazing experience. Suddenly I said to Reg "I feel strange, I'm watching the television, but I can't see anything, I can't hear anything and I'm tingling all over".

It frightened him so much he didn't know what was going on. Just then the phone rang, it was Tony, he never phoned after nine o'clock but he felt that he just had to. I told him what was happening right then as he was talking to me.

I could breathe normally after weeks of gasping for breath, no asthma. Reg and I cried into each other's arms and that night I threw all the pillows out of the bed and laid down for the first time for months. I slept for nine hours that night, the first good night's sleep I had had for months, no not months, years. No more breathalysers, no more nebulisers, no more pills. I felt wonderful, I was not at all afraid of what was to come. I knew that the Lord was in my corner. If the Lord wanted to take me, I was ready. If He wanted me to remain then that too would be OK, more than OK.

Reg and I went to church on the Sunday morning to have prayers said for us, everyone gave me a hug and I felt wonderfully happy, not at all in fear or apprehension. When I went into hospital that same evening, there was a young girl of about seventeen curled up sucking her finger in the bed next to mine. I sat and talked to her. She said that her mother had died two months earlier and her Dad lived 150 miles away, she was all alone and she was terrified. I hugged her to my chest, and we cried in each other's arms. I promised that I would be her Mum whilst she was in hospital and would take care of her.
We said prayers together with my Ann and she became quite calm as they took her down for her emergency surgery. I was there when she came back. I soothed her,

bathed her hands and face, stroked her hair until she fell asleep. After that she wanted to be with me all the time.

Looking around the ward, I saw people sitting by themselves or trying to read or looking out of the window. No one seemed to be talking to each other, I would soon change that. The next morning, I went around chatting to everyone and introducing them to each other so that they could have someone to talk to instead of just sitting on their own worrying about themselves. Then it was time to prepare me for my operation. I said a little prayer thanking the Lord for all he had done for me and placing myself into his hands. I went down to the theatre quite calm and at peace. Someone was calling my name, "Margaret wake up" it was the nurse at my side. I opened my eyes and saw at the end of my bed my lovely daughter, her face was framed with flowers, she was smiling with tears rolling down her cheeks. "Mum" she said "It wasn't malignant". I said "O" and went back to sleep. Reg had phoned the hospital to see how I was but they would only tell him that I was all right. He still didn't know that the cancer wasn't malignant.

My Ann belted round to her dad's to tell him the good news. They fell into each other's arms with tears running down their faces. I think that was the first time in ages that Reg had had a good sleep, knowing that I would be coming home again. Each day I got stronger and had made many friends whilst I was in hospital. I had to be moved to another ward where there was only one other lady, because in the next bed to me was an old lady who talked and talked all night, and slept all day. She talked very loud because she was hard of hearing, and in the bed the other side of me was a lady who had her family visiting all day, they were a very nice loving family, they came straight after breakfast and didn't leave until supper time, and they talked and laughed all the time. I knew everything about that family, even the colour of their curtains and carpets. So that was why I was moved.

It was lovely to have some peace and quiet at night, I didn't get much peace during the day though, because the people in the ward I was moved from came to see me, that was nice though because I was getting my sleep at night, and I like people, and I like to talk, as any of my friends will tell you.

The evening before I was due to come home, I had visitors from the other ward. I was telling them about this book I had written, this book about my life for the benefit of my family. The more I told them, the more they wanted to hear. Gradually more and more people came until there were eight people sitting around me, they pulled the chairs up, and sat on the bed. It's a good job that the ward was almost empty because everyone was laughing and interested in what I had to stay. Usually at about nine o'clock everyone would settle down for the night and go to sleep, but this night no one wanted to go. Eventually the nurses came to see what all the laughing was about, told us to be quiet, but they stayed to listen. It was eleven o'clock, and even I had had enough for now, so we all retired to our own beds.

Ann picked me up on the following Sunday and took me home, she was coming back at 4.30 to cook our Sunday dinner and in the meantime Reg and I could enjoy being together on our own. Reg put on my favourite George Gershwin disc and we two danced gently together with our arms around each other with the tears running down our cheeks, just happy that it was all over. All we did all afternoon was talk and hug each other with the tears always present. Reg couldn't stop holding me, just as if I was going to disappear.

I am typing this just three days after my op and the most important thing that has happened to me in my life is the wonder of The Lord. When all else fails, pray to the Lord, He is the one who loves us the most, He is the only one who can perform miracles. "Thank you, Lord, for all you have done for me".

CHAPTER 29
Our Fiftieth Anniversary

The previous part of my story could well have been my last episode. Since writing it I have more to tell because I am still here to do so.

Reg and I had our fiftieth wedding anniversary coming up, this was a special day and we didn't want to do the usual birthday celebration which was going out with all the family for a meal because you couldn't really talk to each other sitting at a long table with half your family at the other end. So, we decided that we would have the party at Ann's house, she has a large house with plenty of room, and a large dining room. Ann said leave it to me, I will arrange everything, and she did.

On the day, Reg and I were supposed to go around immediately after lunch, all the family would be there, and we would spend the rest of the day together enjoying chatting and laughing together.

Ann and Tony cooked up one surprise after another. First of all, they had arranged for the cook of the year who won the award on television to come and wait on us and prepare our meal. She brought her husband with her to wait on us all throughout the afternoon, with drinks and sweetmeats, and little savoury snacks, it was delightful, and they were such a pleasant couple.

We all selected what we wanted to eat beforehand, and we had a feast. The flowers in the lounge and dining room were so beautiful. Halfway through the afternoon it was present time. We had some lovely gifts from all the family, and whilst I was opening them my Ann called out "Mum". I looked up and there before me were my friends Rose and Ron who I hadn't seen for years because we had all been too poorly to travel all the long way which took five hours by road to see each other. We rushed into each other's arms, crying and hugging (My Tony was very busy with his camera) he caught every precious moment on film.

The family were all gathered around me with my very best friend since I was sixteen to present me with – My Story-. I had been writing this story for a year, I had no computer, so most of it was written by hand. My daughter had put it onto her computer but let me tell you from the beginning how it came to be made into a book.

In the beginning I decided that my family ought to know where they came from, especially the younger members. All the good things, and home comforts that they now have and take so much for granted. These things have come to pass because of all the hard work that Reg and I have done in our lives.

CHAPTER 30
My Brushes with People in Danger

I want them to know that they shouldn't be afraid to show their love for each other all the time, plenty of hugs and kisses, holding hands whilst watching the television, little things that show that you care for each other. Talk things over, don't harbour a grudge, it you are not happy about something talk about it quietly together. Never go to bed at night if you have had an argument without a hug.

Sometimes during our lifetime, I would get all het up and cross, but you could never have an argument with Reg, he would just walk away. I would work furiously, tidying up, polishing and hoovering until I got it out of my system, then Reg would come up behind me, give me a kiss, and say "Do you want a cup of tea love?". How can you continue to be cross with anyone like that?

Tony and Ann had arranged with each other that they would get my story made into a book, not by a printer or publisher, but by themselves. So, whilst we were away for the week-end visiting Tony, Ann came to our bungalow and raided our photo albums for pictures. This book with a large picture of me when I was eighteen completely filling the front cover(it was the picture Reg carried around with him during the war) was presented to me at the party, and there was a copy for all the family, and one for my dear

Rose, who Ann had invited to stay with her for the week-end. The pictures I have of me receiving the book are of me crying my eyes out, not sad tears, but joyful tears. Everyone came and gave me a big hug. My son Tony held me and said "I love you very much Mum, I am so proud of you".

My Ann cried with me, everyone was crying, this was supposed to be a happy celebration, and there we all were crying. My grandson Iain took his Dad's copy and began to read it straight away, he was nine years old, he didn't put it down until he had read it right through. My friend Rose took hers to bed with her, and read it right through before she went to sleep in the early hours of the morning. She told me that she read it again as soon as she got home, and by now all her family have read it, and her friends.

I mentioned to a few of my friends in church that I had written the story of my life, and they asked if they could read it. This book of mine has been passed from hand to hand until almost every member of my church, and their families have read it. I have a waiting list of people waiting to read it, some want to read it again. Some shopkeepers somehow got to find out about it, and have read it also. Some people have asked me to write some more about my life because they are so interested, especially the younger ones. So here I am adding some more of my life.

I would like to tell you about the people who I have helped along the way. There was the young man in hospital who I hope I saved from being lacerated by flying glass. There was my daughter Ann who I nursed through scarlet fever when she was only a baby.

I used to like to go swimming and one day I went to the local indoor pool. I was the only one there having a swim apart from a few mums and toddlers in the far end in the babies' pool. I had got out to have a rest, and was sitting on the seat at the side when a little boy, about five years old, came running out of the gents changing rooms which happened to be right in the centre of the pool, and of course in the deep water part. He threw himself into the water, I watched thinking he must be a very good swimmer for his age, but no, he couldn't swim, he had gone under and hadn't come up. I quickly jumped in and brought him out, I pumped the water out of him until he revived and ran off to the toddler's pool.

Where was the lifeguard who was always on duty sitting on a high chair at the side of the pool? I was furious. He came wandering back, and when I confronted him, he said "I have only been gone ten minutes, and there was no one in the pool then". "Where is this boy then?" he asked. So, I took him to show him the little lad who confirmed what I had said. If I hadn't been there, that little boy wouldn't be here today. I suppose I should have reported him, but he swore that he would never leave the pool unattended again, he was really scared at what might have happened.

We were coming back from a holiday in Cornwall when we landed in a traffic jam on the Exeter Bypass. There were no motorways there all those years ago. There were three lines of traffic packed together like sardines, it went on for miles. We were in the outside lane Reg and me, stopped with the handbrake on. The traffic coming from the other direction was running quite fast, there was no hold up there. All of a sudden there was an almighty bang. A motor bike had come up on the white line in the middle of the road and had panicked when he saw the traffic coming towards him. He had hit the back part of my car which threw his bike across the road slicing off the wheels of a car which carried a family of four and a dog, with camping equipment on the roof. Their car ploughed off the road with no wheels. The bike was thrown back onto my car on impact straight into my door. Both riders, a boy and a girl, were thrown off onto the oncoming traffic. I didn't hesitate, I couldn't get out of my door because it was buckled, so I climbed over Reg (who was sitting shocked) and got out of his door and ran to pull the girl into the safety of the front of my car. The boy staggered to safety, only just in time, I felt the wind as cars rushed past me. The girl didn't appear to have any broken bones but was unconscious. I was amazed when an ambulance pulled up and took her to hospital within a few minutes of the accident. Apparently, they had just picked up another traffic accident victim, and were on their way back to hospital. You know we are all supposed to have a guardian angel watching over us, I wonder if that young girl's guardian angel used me to save her, to this day I can't believe what I did.

Another time, I took Ann to the seaside when she was a young girl. We were on the promenade watching the world go by when all of a sudden, we saw a little girl washed off of a concrete pier that was running down to the sea. It was so sudden, the waves were getting bigger and bigger every minute, nobody seemed to be doing anything. I ran as fast as I could shouting all the time, I ran to the end of the pier where the little girl had disappeared and jumped in. She was all right once I got her out, but it was a near thing, that undercurrent nearly got me as well. You know I had almost forgotten about this incident until Ann reminded me.

Then there was the young man who had cut an artery in his arm which was spurting out, I was able to stop the blood by holding the vein together until the ambulance arrived. And, of course, my son Tony who I saved from drowning whilst we were on holiday. Seven people, my life is worthwhile after all.

CHAPTER 31
Our Super Holiday

Reg and I hadn't had a proper holiday for a very long time, because I have been ill on and off for years, so we decided to treat ourselves to celebrate our golden wedding. We booked up to go on a cruise around the Mediterranean Sea. Now if you remember I said that I couldn't go on the sea because of the time I nearly drowned when I was a toddler, but I said to myself, if the Lord wanted me to die, I wouldn't be here now so I would chance it. We had a wonderful time and met a lot of very nice people.

I said earlier on that I liked to talk, well each day when we sat out on the sun deck people would join each other at the tables and pass the time of the day enjoying the sun and chatting. I couldn't resist telling them of the wonders that had happened to me in my life, of how the Lord had intervened on numerous occasions especially the healing of my frozen shoulder, and the very last one of bringing me safely through the operation for cancer. After a few days, even strangers who I hadn't even spoken to, were calling out "Good morning Margaret" or were coming to sit next to me and chat as if we were old friends. There were a couple who came and sat with me when I went to an afternoon tea dance on my own, they were Swedish and had heard about me and wanted to know more. I couldn't get away from them and we were talking for three hours, Reg thought that I had got lost.

It's strange but by the end of the first week everybody was talking to each other, I have never met so many nice people at one time. When our holiday came to an end, I was glad that I had spread the word of the Lord, for look how happy it had made everyone, so this is how I will end my story.

CHAPTER 32
My Five weeks Waiting for Triple By-Pass
and My Book is Published

Whilst I was in hospital, this book was being printed so I
decided to add some more
because it is more of my life story.

I was leading up to a heart attack, I didn't know anything
about it but as I was cleaning my car I felt dizzy and faint,
so I stopped and went indoors and sat down.

I had a cup of tea and, when I felt better, I went out and
finished cleaning the car.
I didn't take any more notice of it, I didn't dream that I was
going to have a serious thing wrong with me.

When I got up the next morning, it was about 7 o'clock, I
made a cup of tea and was sitting down in the front room
when all of a sudden I felt really funny and my arm went
dead, then all my right side went dead and I fell to the floor.
I was sick and I couldn't move. The pain in my chest was
awful, I said to Reg "go and phone for the ambulance
quickly". I was just lying there, I managed to put myself in
the recovery position and it wasn't very long before the
ambulance came. The ambulance station is just down the
bottom of our road which is fine because they got to us
quickly.

When Reg was on the 'phone speaking to the emergency services, he said to the operator "Don't keep talking to me and asking me questions, please send the ambulance". She said "They are listening to this conversation and they are on their way to you now" then the doorbell rang, it was as quick as that.

They got me into the ambulance and kept me there for about half an hour, I was so cold I was shivering; they were resuscitating me and doing all sorts of things to me. They put me on oxygen.

We went to the Bristol hospital, they rushed me into the emergency department to look after me, and I don't remember a lot of this because I was half unconscious. When I came to, there was a doctor and quite a few nurses standing around my bed. The doctor asked me a question, he said "I know you have a lot of pain, you are very ill, you have had a heart attack in your home and you have had another one since you arrived here." He said "I can give you this injection", then he showed me a cylinder, quite a big one about six inches long. He said "If I give you this injection it will stop the pain but it will make you bleed and if the blood goes to your head you will be left paralysed for the rest of your life. There is a 50/50 chance that it will do some good, otherwise I can't say any more about it. You have to sign this form to show that you agree to having the treatment". I didn't know if I was coming or going, I just wanted to get rid of the pain, so I signed the form and he gave me the injection. I wondered why all these people were there, the nurses, the ward manager (who I knew afterwards was called Roger) and the doctor. The pain went away and I went to sleep.

When I woke up, I asked to have a bed pan. I filled it up, there was a lot of blood in it but I am still here today so obviously it did the trick. They kept me in the Emergency ward for 5 days. I would like to stop there for a second; I need to go back a little bit because I would like to say that my daughter Ann was wonderful, every time I opened my eyes she seemed to be there. My son Tony had to come a long way and he came straight away, it was a terrible time for all my family.

The ward manager, Roger, looked after me himself. I think he took a shine to me for some reason, some old lady he didn't know, and he seemed to want to care for me. One time whilst I was there, I bought up some sick which got lodged in my throat. I couldn't breathe, fortunately Ann was with me and Roger was just behind fiddling with all the gadjets that I was wired up to. She said "Quick, my mum can't breathe" so he got a tube down my throat so that he could clear it and I could breathe again. I was in a panic, I thought that I was really going to die that time.

People who had a heart attack came to this emergency room but they only stayed perhaps for a few hours, or a day and a night, then they were transferred to a ward. I was there for five days which was unusual, Roger just wouldn't let me go, and he wanted to make sure that I was alright.

They brought the X ray machine to my bed because I was unable to get up. The next day they took me to have an Angiogram, this is when they put a tube into a vein in your groin which has a camera attached so that they can see what is happening inside, all clever stuff. Before I went to have this done, a friend of mine who works in the hospital, called Marlene, knew I would be going to have this done so she was there waiting for me in the corridor and we said a prayer together holding hands.

They took me in, they put me on a slab, and it was quite high up. Everyone was busy preparing me, nobody was talking to me and I was scared, I was really afraid and was trembling. At this point I just called to the Lord and said "I need you now, I need you to see me through this" Immediately I stopped shaking, I was alright. The Doctor said "I am going to put this into your groin, it might hurt a bit but we have got to keep you awake so that we can do this properly." He started and I didn't feel any pain. I was looking up at the television set watching and I said to the Doctor "It's a shame it isn't in colour" It goes to show how relaxed I was after being so nervous.

They took me from there back to the emergency room for another day, and then I was transferred to a coronary ward. The ward was a T shape; there was a long strip at one end, then a section in the middle for offices then the other end made the T shape which was where they put me. I was in a bed facing the nurses' station where they sat, so that they could keep an eye on me; well I had had two heart attacks. The nurses gave me something to squirt under my tongue if I felt that I was going to have another heart attack. I would like to tell that I used this twice more while I was there, I had two minor attacks, called to the nurse and used this under my tongue and got over them.

Every day whilst I was in there I would get up and have a shower, get dressed, I was the only one who ever got dressed, everyone else stayed in pyjamas and dressing gowns.

I decided to have a look around, so I wandered up to the other end of the ward, all the beds were occupied by men, the ladies where down at the other end (the T part). Everyone seemed so alone, they didn't seem to be talking to each other which was strange for a place full of people, and it was very full with all the beds taken.

I found out that some of them, mostly men, had been in there for weeks waiting to have a heart operation. I began to think that I am going to be here a long time because I have only just come in and they have been waiting weeks. One lady in the same ward as me had already been there four weeks, the doctor had told me it would be two to three weeks before I could be done, so I knew that I wasn't going to get out of there very quickly. Anyway, each day I got up, had a shower, dressed and went around the ward talking to people. Some of them were only in for a short time having a pacemaker fitted, or a minor operation, I got to know most of them very well.

When I took my morning walk to say good morning to everyone they called out "Morning Margaret". I knew all their names and I became very fond of a lot of them. If somebody didn't have any visitors I would go and chat with them and tell them about my life, they were very interested especially the younger ones, they would ask me to tell them mostly about my younger days, about how poor most people were and what a hardship life was then, of course you have already read this at the beginning of my story.

The time drags when you are in hospital so I learnt that people liked to talk about their families and their lives so I would go around and arrange people's flowers, talk to them, introduce them to each other, all sorts of things. The staff nurse in charge of our ward kept telling me off and ordering me back to bed, she said 'You are just as sick as the other people, do as you're told", When Reg came in to see me she told him" I can't control your wife at all, will you talk to her and tell her she has got to go back to bed". He said "I have been trying all my life to tell her what to do and she doesn't take any notice of me''. It's not true really but that's what he said.

I kept myself busy and whenever anybody went down for an operation I would go and wish them luck, give them a kiss and say "I will be here when you come back". I would sit by their bed when they were coming round so that they would know I was there because I just get on with people somehow.

I have got to tell you something. At my church were Eric & Vera Angel. They were very popular, they were just like everyone's best friend. I was regularly on the reception door in church with Eric, he was such a happy soul, and I say was because he is no longer with us. When I was in hospital Eric phoned me every day so that he could tell the rest of my friends how I was progressing, the sister would call across the ward "Margaret, your angel is on the line" and everybody would laugh that I had my very own angel. I had lots of cards, I had so many that I couldn't put them all up behind my bed. Some people came in who had no cards or visitors so I would go and pin up one of my cards behind their bed. As a matter of fact one lady phoned me when she went home and invited me out to lunch with her.

I had been in hospital about three weeks. All the wards were being emptied because the millennium year was coming up (YEAR 2000) the hospital was preparing for an influx of patients at Christmas and the New Year. They brought in a young woman, her name was Carol, and she was 28 years old and had been in and out of hospital for three years having all sorts of tests. They wheeled her in on a bed, she had two nurses with her and had drips and things. The porters were trying to decide where to put her, the ward was half empty, I said "Put her in the bed next to me and I will look after her"

She had come from Bath to have more tests in the Bristol Royal, she was like a skeleton and hadn't been able to get out of bed to go to the toilet or anything, She had all sorts of machines round her monitoring her, she was next to me opposite the nurses' desk so that they could keep an eye on both of us because while I was there I had two more attacks but because I was in hospital and could call for help they didn't turn out to be very dangerous, they gave me my medicine, two squirts under my tongue,

So, I made friends with Carol, I felt so sorry for her, she was tall and thin, painfully thin, she hadn't been able to walk for a long time. The nurses used to lift her out of bed and sit her on a chair so that they could change her bed. I looked after Carol as if she were my own child, we talked a lot and said prayers together, I also arranged for the Chaplain to come up on Sunday to give us communion, Reg was there with us too.

I got so frightened about this girl because one day in particular she had been crying, tossing and turning and really unhappy, so when we had said our prayers that night, I promised her that I would pray for her until I fell asleep, and I did. I said "Please Lord, help this poor young woman Carol, help her before you help me, I have had my time, I just want you to help her, she is only young, she has got two young boys who she hardly sees, please help her Lord". I went to sleep. I didn't get to sleep very early, you can't get much sleep in hospital because there is so much noise going on all the time, the hustle and bustle, new patients arriving, the nurses going about their business, sometimes I would wake up in the early hours of the morning and go and have a chat with the nurses in their quiet period, we would have a cup of tea.

When the next day came, I pulled the curtains back from around our beds and saw that all the machines round Carol had gone, she was sitting up in bed and said she felt fine. During that day she went down to the toilet with a walking frame and a nurse to help her, that's the first time she had been able to do that for ages, so don't you tell me that there isn't a God when prayers are answered like that so quickly.

I truly and honestly believe that miracles do happen.

When I started writing my life story, I did it for my children; I wanted them to know how lucky they are to be living in the world today. Everybody has got so used to the life of luxury that we have, nobody needs to die from lack of food (that is in our England) everybody can have first class medical treatment for free, (not like America and other countries), most families own a car, television, computer. School diners are the norm. I can go on and fill a whole page with things we never used to have when I was a girl.

Anyway, let me get back to my story. You don't want 25O books on your hands! The printers wouldn't do less than that so I decided I must do something about it. I 'phoned the local newspaper and told them about myself and they sent a reporter and a photographer who took some snaps and asked me lots of questions; I just gave them a copy of my book.

The following week I was amazed, when I opened the paper. There was half a page
with a large photograph of me, they hadn't even notified me that it was going to be printed.
I took this to the local book shop with a copy of my book which they decided to sell for me. They had an enlarged picture of the front page in their window.

Lots of friends from church and family bought copies, some people bought more than one, I have lots of letters from people who say that the book is being passed from family to family and I have even had letters from abroad. **Billy Graham's church had a copy which was being read by the congregation so much that the vicar there asked if he could have another because it was getting a bit tattered. By the way Billy Graham is the well know preacher who has been on videos all over the world, his photograph is in this book.**

I live in a little place called Nailsea, it used to be a village but it has now become a small town with all the usual shops, Tesco, Somerfield, Kwiksave, Iceland etc. We are getting more people moving in. I became so well known in our town that it was difficult to go shopping or for a walk without someone wanted to chat with me, I was a local celebrity.

I decided that I would send a copy of my book to the Queen Mother. I phoned the operator to give me the telephone number of Buckingham palace and without hesitation she told me. I 'phoned the palace and asked to speak to the Queen Mother's private secretary, I didn't know that his name was Sir Alistair Aird until the girl on the phone told me. She put me through straight away. The time took about 2 minutes and there I was explaining why I would do such a thing as to offer the Queen Mother the story of my life. Sir Alistair said that he remembered the occasion that I was talking about because he was there and remembered it well; this story is in the first part of my memoirs. The Queen Mother was 98 years old at the time and could hardly see so he said that he would enjoy reading it to her. I got a very nice letter from Buckingham Palace thanking me, which I will treasure. I bet the postman wondered what was up when he saw who the letter was from because the crest was on the envelope.

I heard a little later that the Queen Mother had died, it is very sad but she was an old lady. She was lovely and absolutely charming, I think she was the best of all the royals that I have waited on, most of them, not of course the younger ones because I had gone on to do other things.

I had a 'phone call from the man who **runs the Bristol Hospital radio**, he wanted to interview me on the radio because he had read my book and liked it very much.   I wasn't very well because I was getting over my operation so I had to say no, but he kept phoning me saying "Please, it will be lovely if you could come because the patients would like to hear your story'. So, I said alright and he picked me up and took me there and gave me half an hour, it turned out very well really.

I have got a disc and a tape to keep as a memento. I did make a talking tape for the benefit of my family of the whole story, my son's youngest son Stephen has listened to it at night time when he went to bed, he has already read the book but liked to listen to the tapes before he went to sleep because it is more personal.

I had lots of letters from people and one of my favourites was from June, my nurse from hospital, saying "We would love to see you, why don't you come up and see us?" She asked me to bring some of my books, she already had one but wanted four more for her relatives abroad who wanted to read it. So, I went to see her, I had to walk around the ward seeing all the patients who had heart operations, she told them that I had my operation a few weeks ago and said "Look how well our Margaret is, she never made a fuss". She said "Please come again, we would love to see you, you have helped cheer our patients up". I never went back but I still get messages from her, and cards at Christmas time.

Something else I remember whilst I was in hospital. The lady who came round with the food and drink trolley was a little fat jolly person. I liked to help her, she was full of fun and we used to have a laugh with the patients. On Christmas morning, she brought me a present; it was all wrapped up with pink ribbon and she said "I have bought this for you Margaret then gave me a kiss on the cheek." I think that I have said enough about my time in hospital, I don't want to make my story boring.

The response I have had regarding my story has been fantastic, so many people have said that they would like to see it on the television, comments like it would be great to see how people used to live and what the world was really like, there were rich people, and poor people, not many in-betweens, I could write another book talking about the old days, the days of the war, the heartache of so many people being killed, not only in the forces but at home which should have been a safe place.

CHAPTER 33
I Was a Stand-In for a Child Movie Star

Here are a few incidents I thought you might like to hear
about. When I was about eight years old, I lived next door
to a girl who was my friend. Her auntie came to visit her
while I was playing there, she asked me if I would like to
be in a film because they were looking for somebody to
take the place of the star who was in the film, I was to be a
stand in. The auntie asked my mother if I could go, of
course she said yes especially when she was told that I
would get three pounds and fifty pence for the work (That
is the equivalent of a week's pay at the time).
So, on the day she came to pick me up, my mum had curled
my hair and put on my best dress. I only had two so it
didn't take long to choose and the lady took me on a train to
Elstree studios. They had a big lake; they wanted me to fall
out of a boat holding a piece of sausage in my hand and a
dog would come out to save me. I had to grab hold of its
collar, give it the piece of sausage then the dog would pull
me to the shore. It wasn't very far out but it was too deep
for me to put my feet on the ground. Well you know I
didn't know what I was going to do really but I did hear
somebody say that the lake was frozen over this morning,
huh, and I had to fall into this cold water, anyway I couldn't
do anything about it, I was there, they didn't want me to
have curly hair so they straightened all my curls out. They
put a dress on me that the star would be wearing then I had

to get into this boat and they pushed me out. There was a man standing in the water to save me if I got into trouble, you see I couldn't swim at the time. So, I fell into the water splashing about like mad, then the dog came, had his sausage and pulled me to the beach. Now the beach had all shingles on it which grazed my knees, they made them bleed when the dog pulled me out. They wrapped me in a warm towel and took my clothes to dry, that was when they couldn't find my knickers, so when it was time to go home I had to go with no knickers on, it was a good job it wasn't very cold, anyway my mum was well pleased when I gave her the money.

CHAPTER 34
My Time at Dulwich College for Boys

There was a time when I worked for Dulwich College in the kitchen as an assistant chef.
This college is a very high-class fee paying school which accepts a few free pupils who had passed a scholarship.
My son, Tony, could have gone to the school because he had passed all the qualifications to be admitted.
Unfortunately, they told him that he couldn't go because he wasn't living in the area so he went to another school. He went to the same school that Reg, his dad, went to.
Anyway, I'll get back to the time when I worked at the college.

It was very interesting, there were lots of us in the kitchen, about 2O. The kitchens were spotlessly clean. We used to prepare the meals for the boys, that was hard work because we had sacks full of vegetables to prepare each morning, carrots and cabbages, potatoes and all sorts of stuff.

The boys' favourite meal was shepherd's pie; they used to put everything that was left over, with a few spices, into the mincing machine. Most of the boys stayed at school and were borders who slept in. They would have breakfast every morning and what was left over, bacon, eggs, sausages, meat and vegetable remains, all went into the machine to make this absolutely gorgeous stuff for the shepherd's pie. We put mashed potato on top then baked it till it was all nice and brown and crunchy. The boys loved it, if we didn't have a lot of left overs we couldn't make it and they used to moan like hell because they all wanted some, all of us girls liked it as well.

The boys were very well behaved, they used to form a queue and there was no pushing or fighting, they were nice boys. They were very polite, they could choose what they wanted to eat, there were three different choices of the main meal and three choices for sweets, they did very well.

The headmaster and teachers would sit on a platform at the front of the hall for their meals; they had the same food as everyone else. The lady who served them had to leave so they asked me if I would serve them (they knew that I was a waitress), so I said 'yes I would'. It was supposed to be a privileged thing to do (I never said that I had enjoyed waiting on royalty). So, I worked in the kitchen until lunch time, then I served the staff, cleared their table then helped the rest of the staff to clear up. We all sat down to lunch together, that's when I started to put on weight. I only worked there for six months because that's all I wanted to do; I wanted to learn how to do catering for a lot of people.

I was working for Grayson Caterers at the same time as being a dinner lady, then I could go home after I had finished lunch and could still do my evening work and weddings, parties, all sorts of banquets, cocktail parties, lots of things so that I could earn some money. I thought I would tell you about that because it is quite interesting.

CHAPTER 35
Finding the Grown-Up Child I Saved from
Drowning was One of My Best Friends in Church

Early on in my story I told about a little girl I saved from drowning. When some friends of mine in church read this about the child, they questioned me about it saying "Where did it happen?" "In Cornwall" I replied "It was one on those concrete slipways leading down to the sea". "What was she wearing?" they asked. "A dress" I said. (By the way the lady who asked the questions was called Joyce Leggett, her husband is David and they have two children Stephen and Katie). Joyce said "That was me, I was wearing a swimming costume that looked like a dress because it had a frilly top with a skirt, you're the lady who saved me!" We went into lots of details regarding the time and place when it happened but I still couldn't believe that, because of what I did, here was this family who I have known for fifteen years and have been great friends with. Many times we have enjoyed weekends away with the church, dinner parties, and barbecues. Just think if I hadn't seen Joyce being washed into the sea when she was a little girl, Joyce, David, Stephen and Katie wouldn't be here and this world would have been a lot poorer without this Christian family, it's a small world we live in, isn't it?

CHAPTER 36
Meeting Up with Teenagers in Nailsea

One day at the beginning of November a few years ago, there was a ring at the door, there were four boys, thirteen and fourteen years old, they were making an awful row, I asked 'What are you doing" They said "We're singing a carol". I said "I've never heard that one before". They said "We wrote it ourselves". I told them you'll never make any money like that, that's a shocking noise. I asked them if they knew what date it was, and didn't they know that Christmas was in December, they replied "Well it doesn't matter does it?". I told them of course it matters, if you want to make some money singing carols you had better start practicing. I gave them a copy of my carol sheet from church, none of them went to church, but anyway I gave them a few tips and sent them away to practice.

The following week they were back again, once again the horrible noise, "We've been practising, will you listen to how we have got on?" I said "alright go on and sing". They had learnt one of the carols from the sheet I had given them, it wasn't much better really. I gave them a few more tips and told them to practice some more. They were back again three days later, this time they had two girls with them. I didn't invite them in because I didn't know who they were, and it was a very cold November night. The girls said that they had been practicing around their house, and they had come with them to see who I was.

They knew me because their parents had bought my book; they also had read my story. I gave them a few more tips, we had a chat about various things and away they went.

They came back the following week and I let them rehearse in my front room.
It was getting near Christmas, they came and knocked on the door, there were six of them this time plus the two girls making eight altogether. They said "We are just going out carol singing", I said "Come back and let me know how you got on." They did come back, they had made thirty pounds." They sang for me in my front room and I joined in, they were quite good. I offered them some money which they wouldn't take; instead each of the four boys who had started gave me a large bar of chocolate for helping them.

These boys and girls used to come and see me every week, they were local kids and wanted to ask me questions about what it was like when I was young. We would sit in my dining room and I would tell them stories, I had made a talking book about my life which they liked to listen to.

Over the next few weeks I had more and more children coming in, all the same age group, from the same school. One night I had twelve and, as I have only a two bedroom bungalow, it was much too much. The first children that came were very well behaved, I expect it was because they knew me from reading my book,

I am afraid that I had to stop all of them coming because the late arrivals misbehaved. They wanted something to eat, they wanted a drink, they went to the toilet, they went in and out of the street door, this was mid-winter and they were leaving the door open. I never knew when any of them were coming, they just turned up, they treated my home as if it was some sort of club where they could come and go as they liked. I love children, children of all ages, but Reg and I had to put a stop to this, so we did.

The first boys still came on their way home from school, I didn't mind that, I would give them a drink and we had a chat, they told me how they were getting on at school, they asked my advice about many things. One time they had an essay to write about any old person, of course they had me. The results of the work, from what I had to tell them, gave them top marks.

One day they said that their teacher wanted to know if I would come and talk about my experiences during the war in their history lesson, and would I be prepared to answer questions. I said that I would. I found out that these boys and girls came from quite well to do parents; they had no idea of the way we used to live when I was their age.

They continued to come now and again, one boy came often on a Saturday and he sometimes brought his little sister with him. They liked to help in the garden, his little sister was only six years old, she liked to get her hands dirty helping in the garden while her brother cleaned the car or mowed the lawn.

In the summer time I often had six or more boys and girls come to see me and play in the garden. I have got a large garden, they would lark about doing cartwheels and playing with the hosepipe but they never came in the house when there was a group of them.

I have always liked children as you know from the beginning of my book, I did the mothers' and toddlers' group in my church for years, I only had to stop when I was seventy two because I developed asthma, I couldn't afford to catch a cold from the babies who I played with; it only made my asthma worse.

I invited my young friends to come to our church for a party at Christmas. I said "come and knock for me and we will go together". I couldn't go because I developed a bad cold that triggered off my asthma so they went along without me but came back in half an hour because they didn't know anyone there. I encouraged them to go back again, I had already told my friends in church to make them welcome but they didn't stay long again, back they came to me and we spent a little time together before they went home. I wish that I could have persuaded them to come regularly, they liked to sing and they could have been in our choir.

CHAPTER 37

Remembering Reg's Mums and Dad

I have told many stories about my life, now I want to tell you about Reg's Mum and Dad.

Alice, Reg's mum, was born in 1899. She grew into a beautiful young woman. Ted, Reg's dad, was born in 1896 and they were married when Alice was twenty years old. They had two children Doris and Reg my husband. Alice, I'm not going to call her Alice anymore because to me she was Mum, so Mum she will be for the rest of the chapter.

Mum was one of 13 brothers and sisters because in those days people had very large families, there was no birth control then. Their mum, granny Parker, was a tyrant and stood no nonsense. When the boys got to the age of 14 when they left school, she would throw them out to fend for themselves. Money was tight, and it was with great difficulty that one man could provide for such a large family.

Some of the boys moved in with their newly married sister Alice and Ted. They couldn't turn them away, the youngsters didn't know what to do. Mum bought them their first decent suit so that they could go and look for a job respectfully. My Reg thought that they were his brothers when he came along because they stayed with Ted and Alice until they got married.

Reg's Mum and Dad

I didn't realise when I met Alice, my future mother in law to be, what a difference she was going to make to my life, she was really a wonderful lady, and she would do anything for anybody.

She was the manageress of the canteen at Victoria Station in London. During the war the troop trains would pull in with soldiers, sailors and airmen, who would come in to have a quick cup of tea and a snack before they got on their train. She also did lunches for the office and railway staff. Doris, her daughter, worked there. I also worked there for a short time whilst I was waiting to be posted. Everyone had to go to the job that was allocated by law, I was just hoping that I wouldn't be sent away too far, I was nearly seventeen then.

Everybody called her 'Mum" because she was like a mum, she was kind to everybody, she was strict but kind. I remember one time a young German girl came in for a job, she had just come over to England, still during the war. She was pregnant and had nowhere to live. Mum took her on, made arrangements for somewhere for her to live and gave her a job in the kitchen. She had no parents and had no one to look after her, so mum took her under her wing and when the baby was due, she bought all the baby clothes and arranged for her to go into hospital to have her baby.

Mum always worked hard, she never had much in the way of luxuries, but she could always find enough cash to help others. During the last great war many people were bombed out and mum's house became full of relatives looking for shelter, they slept on mattresses on the floor, females in one room, men in another and the older children who hadn't been evacuated or had come home in another one. (Some children who had been evacuated couldn't stand being away from home and family so the parents had brought them back, regardless of the danger of the bombs). There were lots of times when the electricity and gas were cut off because of the bombs, fires, explosions and all sorts of reasons.

Mum had a large cauldron on the fire at home to cook hot nourishing food for everyone. Did I say that she was a wonderful cook? At this time, whilst she was working at Victoria Station, the power was cut off so she used this cauldron to cook food for the Station master and staff. Don't forget, she only had an ordinary fire with coal and wood to cook with. She cooked all night and porters would come and collect the food at the local station which was Tulse Hill, her house was on the doorstep of the station and it took only fifteen minutes to arrive at Victoria. It shows you what sort of a person she was.

I have already told you a lot about the times I worked with mum so now I will tell you about her older years. She had lived with us for a time, very happily I might add, and then she got this very nice flat in Streatham overlooking the park. It was a warden controlled flat where they could keep an eye on the people. She had a nice view on the first floor and could watch people going past, horse riders and runners, people walking and playing with their dogs, children playing and laughing, the changes of the seasons when the trees would burst into growth and colour, the children knocking the conkers down, she was happy there.

Reg and I would take fish and chips in once a week; we would go straight from work and have a pleasant evening. If there was any kind of sport on the television we would watch, she loved her sport and would get excited like a youngster watching the goals being scored in football, or a great tennis match, at Wimbledon fortnight she would be glued to the box all day.

She was 86 years old when she became ill, she had cancer of the liver and had to go into hospital, she had been ill for quite a long time before they took her to hospital. We were very worried because she got worse and worse. Reg and I went to hospital every night straight from work, Reg from Fleet Street (The Daily Express) me from my job. She liked me to do her hair, give her a wash and tidy the flowers etc, just make her comfortable. I was the first to arrive, Dol her daughter came a little later. One of the sisters said one evening that she wouldn't let anybody touch her, she said 'My daughter will look after me when she comes in". I wasn't her daughter but to me she was a mother, and to her I was a daughter. Sometimes we stayed all night, the nurses brought us tea and biscuits.

We were told that she wouldn't last much longer so all the family came from all over the country to be with her to say our goodbyes. She wasn't really conscious, but we all went in one at a time to talk to her and say our last goodbyes. We stayed until she drifted off in her sleep, she looked really peaceful. Mum was buried next to Ted who had gone a long time before. The chapel in the cemetery was packed with people, the vicar taking the service had never had so many people for an old person before, and it was truly a wonderful send off for Mum.

We went back to mum's flat and met lots of people who knew her and talked and talked about what she had done in their lives. Lots of addresses were gathered from her address book, people we had never heard off. One man was a Salvation Army man who had been visiting her for years and teaching her all about our dear Lord. I had never known mum to go to church except for weddings, Christenings and funerals, and to find that this man was her friend was wonderful, a great blessing.

Mum had a hard life and she enjoyed a good party, she gave lots of them with Ted on the piano and everyone would get up and 'do a turn'. She had one last little trick up her sleeve. Dol and Reg were looking for a letter or something she had written, she had no bank account, no savings stashed away. They searched but found nothing. Reg Said "Come on mum tell us where it is hidden" and then they found an envelope underneath a paper lining in a drawer. It held a letter explaining what she wanted, she left each of us something, and I had a ring and some imitation pearls which I had admired for their colour years before. Each of the grandchildren had savings accounts kept by her grandson's wife Irene. Then there was a thousand pounds in cash to pay for her funeral. Mum's legacy wasn't money, it was love and memories. You are sorely missed mum, love you.

I must tell you a little bit about Ted my father in law, he also came from a large family. Their mother couldn't afford to keep them all so Ted was sent to a home for boys, a bit like an orphanage, lots of boys whose parents were poor would have to do this, Ted went home for weekends sometimes.

They taught him music; he could play all sorts of instruments, the trumpet and piano being his favourites.

This was the First World War 1914 to 1918. He was sent to fight abroad, first of all he went to Dardanelles, God it was a massacre out there. Then he was taken to Egypt, more fighting, then to France for the rest of the war. It's a miracle that a young boy like that ever came home, just think children these days have only just left school at the age he was when he joined up.

Whilst writing this I have reached the grand old age of 78, I have a lot to be thankful for, two children, four grandchildren and now a great granddaughter who is a wonderful child called Isabel May, and what do you think, her name is May, the same as my lovely cuddly Nan who brought me into the world with her own hands and took care of me throughout my life.

Life isn't easy for me now. I have asthma and arthritis which makes it difficult to do all the things I want to do. Reg is 81 and without him I don't know how I could carry on. You know as you get older it's not your mind that slows down, inside you still think you're not old and try to do things you shouldn't do, like the time when I was 65 and climbed onto our roof to see where it was leaking and yes I did find out.

When I was 65 I was baptised in my church that is Southfield Church in the same road where I live. I needed to be baptised because I was never Christened as a baby and I wanted to confirm that I loved the Lord with all of my heart. Without my church and the lovely people who go there, I would give up the will to live, they have seen me through hard times when I have been ill and depressed because I couldn't do what I wanted to do.

Reg and me aged 80

CHAPTER 38
My Reg is Taken Ill

I am coming to the end of my story now. I would like to tell you of the last two years Reg and I have been together. Do you every have the feeling when you've got children, that you've got a sixth sense when something is wrong? Well this happened to me and Reg. Now Reg never got a cold but one day two years ago he wasn't feeling well and he went to bed early, at 7o'clock. He didn't have any dinner. I was a bit anxious but thought perhaps he has a cold coming. Well during the night I just felt I had to get up and look at him. When I saw him, he was burning up. He was lying in an awkward position and making funny noises, not snoring, but funny noises. This concerned me a lot, so I phoned the doctor. The doctor came and said "we had better get him to hospital right away". He sent for an ambulance and we went to the Bristol Royal Infirmary, the main hospital in Bristol.

He had lots of tests while he was there, and they pronounced that he had pneumonia. It was a very worrying time. My daughter was there of course, she always comes when I call her. We stayed with him until it was sorted out. They put him in intensive care for a couple of days, so I stayed with him most of the time. Anyway, he got better and they let him go after a week. I took him home to look after him. It was very hard to look after someone who has not been ill before. He wasn't used to it and didn't understand what was going on, but he gradually got better and was able to get up and wash. I helped him to get dressed and sort him out, but he wasn't the same Reg. He kept forgetting things and was confused.

Ann

Over the next few months we had to go backward and forwards to hospital to have tests and all sorts of things done. In the meantime, he had a big sore come up on his head.

They sent us to a clinic where they treated people with skin disorders, this was in Bristol again, which meant a long journey. It was most awkward because I couldn't breathe very well. I have had asthma for the last 15 years, and for the last few years it's been acute. I found it difficult to go backwards and forwards because it took the whole day. We went a couple of times a week for tests and x- rays. After 6 months we saw a nice lady who said, "have we taken a swab of this?" and I said no. So, she took the swab and I had a phone call a few days later to say it was MRSA. Now, this is ridiculous really isn't it? All that time and not taking a swab, so we had to be very careful how to handle the thing. I used to go backwards and forwards to hospital for a long time. I was looking after him at home all the time myself. My daughter came around often, but I had him twenty-four hours a day.

We struggled along but things didn't get any better. Reg started losing weight. He was going from a handsome man I married to an old man with a bent back and thin. I found this very hard to take in, but I continued to look after him. Anyway, eighteen months went by and we were asked to go back to hospital again. He had to go in a tube to examine his whole body. The results were not good. They told me he had a tumour on the side of his head. The other side of his head was dead because there was no blood getting to it. So, he had got Alzheimer's. He had blood clots in his lungs. He has anaemia. His heart got weak and he had diverticulitis, something to do with the bowel. I found out about this after it burst tree times, and all the filth and muck had gone everywhere. They couldn't give him an operation for this because he was too old and weak to stand it, so we struggled on.

I got so fed up with going backwards and forwards to treatment rooms and hospital to have the wound on his head treated, I decided to do it myself. I had throw away gloves,

243

the disinfectant, dressings and everything else and just kept it clean. One time when I was cleaning and dressing his wound, he went limp. I eased him to the floor. His eyes were open, but his heart had stopped. Just imagine a lady of eighty-one kneeling down, resuscitating an old man of eighty four and winning. Reg was still here. Reg was the ninth person I have saved. The wound just wouldn't heal up so we carried on, then just before Christmas I went down with a very bad asthma attack and was taken to hospital. My daughter moved in and looked after Reg.

CHAPTER 39
I was taken to Hospital

I was taken to BRI. I couldn't breathe, I was on oxygen.
They put me on a ward with three old ladies. Now these
three old ladies all had dementia or Alzheimer's. They dint
know what they were doing, where they were or anything.
The sort of person I am, I look after people and I would get
up and looked after them, take them to the loo and see to
their needs. At night I would wipe their faces with one of
those face wipes, and then wipe their hands with
disinfectant. Everybody had a jar of disinfectant at the end
of the bed. I used to tuck them in and kiss them goodnight,
each one. One old lady thought she was in a hotel and said,
"would you take me up to bed when it's time to go?" I said
"of course". They used to talk nonsense with me, and I just
agreed with everything they said. Anyway, I turned my
back one day, and this old lady got out of her bed and got
into my bed. I said, "what are you doing?" and she said, "I
like this bed better than mine". I said, "they are all the
same" and she said "no they not, this is the best bed in the
hotel." Anyway, we got her out of bed and back to her
own.

A little while later she was in my locker and I said, "what
are you looking for?' and she said, "I am looking for my
handbag." I said, "It won't be in my locker it will be in

yours." So, I took her back to her bed and got her handbag out of her locker. This sort of thing carried on all the time.

One night there was a lot of commotion from another ward, people were running about and someone was screaming. This woke the ladies up. It was the early hours of the morning, so they started complaining, "I want this, I must go to the toilet.' Trying to get out of bed, the lady next to me had taken all her clothes off. She had bars up the side of her bed and she got her legs through the bars and tried to get out of bed. I was frightened she would break her legs on the bars, so I got to the door. There were two men sitting in the nurses' section and I called for help. Nobody took any notice of me, so I shouted, "One of you better come now". This man, who must have been in his forties, came back with me, he was really angry and he said, "I've got seventy-eight patients to look after, not people like you!" and I thought what am I doing in hospital if I am not a patient? Anyway, he pushed me to the floor. I knocked my face on the end of the bed and knocked my front tooth out. Now, fortunately that front tooth was a crown. He said, "If you don't get up, I'll have to get a hoist to lift you back to bed." I thought to myself, I am not that heavy, I am only ten and a half stone. Surely, he could have given me a hand but, no, he left me on the floor. I crawled over to my bed and managed to pull myself on it. He went back to the lady with her legs sticking out of the bars, telling her off. He laid her down in the bed and covered her naked. I couldn't breathe. I was gasping for breath in bed. He came back to me with oxygen and got my machine working. He hurt my mouth. The nurses came to try and get me to breathe properly. I was really desperate for breath. I just couldn't get any air into me and, all of a sudden, I heard a nurse say "we're losing her, we're losing her." She was panicked. I felt quite calm and ready to go and I thought, who are they losing? Oh, it's me, and took a gasp and I breathed again. That young nurse saved my life, because if she hadn't been there I wouldn't be here today. It was just her calling out that brought me to myself. I found out later that she went to university and only came in one night a week, just to see how things go on in the hospital. I thought well, God must have been moving in mysterious ways again, he was there for me, because if she hadn't been there, I wouldn't be here.

Anyway, to carry on with my story. They brought in another old lady who wouldn't eat or drink, she didn't speak or open her month for two days. I tried to feed her but had no response, her food was taken away uneaten. The third day I forced her mouth open and saw her tongue was swollen so badly she couldn't speak. She kept tapping her throat. I called a young intern doctor and told him to call the ear, nose and throat doctor, which he did. Straight away the doctor put her on a drip and antibiotics and took her to intensive care. He said that I had saved her life, so that was another one on my list. I stayed one more week, looking after the old ladies. I wanted to come home but couldn't until I could breathe into one of those breath measures, whatever they are called, to see that it came up enough for

247

me to go home. So, I did my very best and they let me home the next day.

Of course, Ann was there again to look after me. I wasn't well yet, but we carried on until Christmas when Reg went down with pneumonia again. I thought, oh no. I phoned for the doctor who confirmed pneumonia. I said "'No, you're not taking him to hospital again, last time he went to hospital he got everything wrong with him. I will look after him at home, and I did." The doctor said "he is seriously ill". "I said "I don't care, I am going to look after him at home," and I did. The doctor said he would give me some antibiotics and medicine for him. I asked if we could just let him go to sleep. I said "we have had such a time of it this last year, now it's going to get worse, he's got pneumonia again. Must we put him through this again?" The doctor said "yes we must, it's against the law not to." I said "suppose I don't give him the medicine." He said "You'll be punished if you don't look after him." So, I had to give him the medicine. He got better, but I was still on my own looking after him. Sometimes I had to change the bed twice a night because he sweated and it was hard to get him to eat and drink anything and look after him properly. Anyway, we got there, bit by bit. I was gradually getting worse, my pelvis had gone now, worn out with all the lifting and work. So, I carried on, it was all very hard and I was getting stressed out, but Reg was up and about now. He wanted to go back to bed each day after I washed him, but I wouldn't let him. I made him get dressed and sit in the front room or lay on the settee if he wanted to, which he did, he slept a lot.

After a bit we got a letter from the hospital again to say they wanted Reg to come in for a six-month checkup, so we went back to the hospital. By this time, we couldn't get there on our own. I had to get transport to take us. We got to the hospital much too early and had to hang around waiting to be seen. They did see us early and we were surprised, because there was nobody else in the waiting room when we arrived. A lady came in and took him for his x-ray and said, "we might as well start as you are here". So, he had the x ray and they took him to another room to test his blood and everything. He came back and said they took two x-rays. I said "that's strange, never mind, perhaps the first one didn't come out properly." They said "the doctor will be here soon and you will be first to see him". It was filling up with people by this time, everybody was coming for two o'clock appointments. The doctor came and called out Reg's name. In we went and the doctor said, "I want to show you something." He put the x-rays on the wall with a light behind them. They were big x- rays. The first one had a white mark on the lung as big as a fist. The doctor said "this was taken six months ago and this next one is the one we took today." It was clear. He said "I can't explain what's happened. I just don't know, I've never seen this before." I said "I can tell you what's happened doctor, my daughter's church, my son's church, my church and my friends were praying for Reg to get better and the lord was listening. He has been for most of

my life, I didn't know it in the beginning, but I do now."
He looked at me and said, "well I believe you're right
because there is no other explanation for this."

I was thinking of a time when my grandson, Stephen, my
son's youngest son, said to me "I asked my teacher to pray
for granddad because he wasn't well and she said 'yes we
will pray at the end of the lesson' so, they did". Stephen
went out into the playground and his friends came up to
him. He's got lots of friends by the way, he is a very
popular boy at his school. They said, "We're going to ask
our churches to pray for your granddad as well on Sunday."
So how many people were praying for Reg on that
Sunday?, I can't say but it's fantastic and I believe every
word of it.

Iain and Stephen at Primary school

Carrying on with my story, things never got any better and I had been looking after Reg now for two years. He got worse and worse. You know people with Alzheimer's, they are like little boys or girls. They don't know what they are doing or how to do it. They have to be told everything, and five minutes later they don't remember what you said. They ask questions over and over again. The same question and you answer it as best you can the first four or five times, then you can get a little bit irritable and fed up because you can't keep on all day answering the same questions. Then eventually he would put a hand on my shoulder and say "Look love, you think you have answered my questions, but you haven't, your losing your memory, just tell me this once." So, I tell him again and describe everything he wanted to know. He says," There you are, thank you" and he would turn around and say "oh by the way, I just want to ask you a question" and I would get the same question again, and that's when I felt like screaming. Once it was so bad, I had a very bad day with him, all day, that I went to the top of my garden. I have a big garden, and screamed, just to let it out of me. Now I have something to say that's not very nice. Sometimes it is so bad, the funny things he did, hiding things which you never find again and cutting things up. I thought he had once cut up all my cards that I had in my wallet. No, he hadn't, he took the wallet and hid it. I never found it until my son's family came down from Knutsford, and they were washing up for me after a meal and putting stuff away in the cutlery drawer. There it was at the back of the drawer. How did it get there? No, Reg didn't put it there and all the cards were in it. I had to replace all the cards because this was months later. A lot of things have gone missing which I've never found again. I can't understand how people do this, but of course he had Alzheimer's and didn't know what he was doing. He liked cutting things up and I felt so sorry for the man I love, I've always loved, sixty-three years we had been together. And now he was just a weak old man with no energy left, just eating and sleeping and doing the best he could. Sometimes I'm sorry to say, I got so aggravated with the stupid things he did or questions he asked, I shouted at him. I have never shouted at him in my life, and because I shouted at him it made me cry. I didn't cry because of that, I cried because I loved him. It's so hard to carry on like this but I was still there.

Now I was back in hospital at Christmas, three in a room same as before and when I was there one of the nurses took a liking to me and used to come and chat with me. She said, "Do the social services people come and see you?" I said "No, I've never asked anybody to come and help, we manage the best we can on our own." She said" You ought to contact social services, they will be able to do something for you, I am sure." So, she sent for them and they came and saw me in hospital. They spoke to me for a long time and said, "when you come home, we are coming to see you." So when I came home, after a week they came to see me and went through all my details and said, "You should have asked for help ages ago, you shouldn't have carried on like this on your own, it's ridiculous " They have given me

252

lots of help for which I am grateful. Reg had help in the mornings with his washing and dressing and helpers made our beds. We had a sitter who came for three hours on a Monday morning to give me a chance to go out shopping. It was such a relief to get out of the house.

Did I tell you we both have wheelers to walk with? Every day we walked up to the shops. We went up and down the supermarket aisle to get some exercise. My daughter bought the walkers. Mine has a seat on it so if I get caught out, when my back plays up, I just sit down on it. Sometimes the pain shoots down my legs, my legs give way and I fall over. I get covered with bruises. So, if I've got something to hold onto when I am out, its much safer. Reg had got one because he was much weaker and couldn't walk far without it. So, we both managed to get out of the house for some exercise.

It was now 2008, Reg and I had been together for sixty-five years. We worked hard and loved one another and for all that time Reg has always treated me as if we were still courting. We never said anything nasty or swore, and even today I still love him. Alright, I admit I shouted sometimes recently, it's made me cry to do so. You can ask anyone who lives with Alzheimer's, it's like living with a child who has lost its memory.

The funny thing about this, we played our kind of music a lot and Reg knew all the words. He was happy in a little world of his own, one day he wanted me to dance with him when it was only 8 o'clock in the morning. I was his carer, that's official, and I continued to look after him.

We had an anniversary card form the Queen on our 60th. The postman came in a little red van, he had a smart uniform with a special delivery written on his cap. "I don't get many of these to deliver madam, congratulations." It was a lovely card with gold tassels and a photo of Her Majesty, who I have served quite often in my lifetime.

I have had a full life, it's been rich in many ways. I have a wonderful daughter Ann, she isn't just wonderful to us, her mum and dad, she is kind and considerate and forever doing a good turn for somebody. She is a wonderful mother to our grandchildren and many's the time when Reg and I have needed her she has moved in with us and slept on the floor for a week at a time. I have a son, Tony, who has grown into a loving father and caring son. He lives and works away and comes to see us when he can   He phones two or three times a week to make sure we are all right.

I have four grandchildren. My daughter has John and Emma and my Son has two boys, Iain and Stephen.

Ann's son John is married to a lovely lady Karen, they have my great grandchildren, Isabel and Jake and Ann's daughter Emma gave birth to Robbie who is so wise for his young age. We have lots of get together meals all through the year.

I have a second family, that is my church. Many happy times we have spent together, barbecues, picnics, weekends away with the whole church joining in, sharing each other's company in our homes with Bible classes, visiting each other when help was needed, happy times worshipping together and singing. So many times, I have asked for prayers and they have never let me down.

Reg with Ann, Emma, Karen, Isabel and Me

When I started to write my story, it was for my family, to let them know how lucky they are to be alive today, but now I feel that the story could be a way to make everyone glad with what they have.

Yours with Love

Margaret Lawrence

Made in the USA
Middletown, DE
30 June 2022